HEAVEN

&

HELL

ARE THEY REAL?

CHRISTOPHER D. HUDSON

THOMAS NELSON
Since 1798

NASHVILLE   DALLAS   MEXICO CITY   RIO DE JANEIRO

Published in Nashville, Tennessee, by Thomas Nelson. Thomas Nelson is a registered trademark of HarperCollins Christian Publishing, Inc.

Unless otherwise noted, Scripture quotations are taken from the Holy Bible, New International Version®, NIV®. Copyright © 1973, 1978, 1984, 2011 by Biblica, Inc.™ Used by permission of Zondervan. All rights reserved worldwide.

Scripture quotations marked NKJV are from the New King James Version. Copyright © 1982 by Thomas Nelson, Inc. Used by permission. All rights reserved.

Scripture quotations marked NLT are taken from the *Holy Bible*, New Living Translation. © 1996. Used by permission of Tyndale House Publishers, Inc., Wheaton, Illinois 60189. All rights reserved.

Scripture quotations marked MSG are taken from *The Message* by Eugene H. Peterson. © 1993, 1994, 1995, 1996, 2000. Used by permission of NavPress Publishing Group. All rights reserved.

Scripture quotations marked TLB are taken from *The Living Bible*. © 1971. Used by permission of Tyndale House Publishers, Inc., Wheaton, Illinois 60189. All rights reserved.

Scripture quotations marked GW are taken from the God's Word translation. Copyright © 1995 by God's Word to the Nations. Used by permission of Baker Publishing Group.

Scripture quotations marked ESV are taken from the English Standard Version. © 2001 by Crossway Bibles, a division of Good News Publishers.

Scripture quotations marked NASB are taken from the New American Standard Bible®. © The Lockman Foundation 1960, 1962, 1963, 1968, 1971, 1972, 1973, 1975, 1977, 1995. Used by permission.

Quotes taken from: WHAT'S THE TRUTH ABOUT HEAVEN AND HELL? Copyright © 2013 by Douglas A. Jacoby Published by Harvest House Publishers Eugene, Oregon 97402 www.harvesthousepublishers.com Used by Permission.

Quotes on page 114–118 by Francis Chan, Copyright 2011 by Francis Chan. *Erasing Hell: What God Said About Eternity and the Things We've Made Up.* Published by David C. Cook. Publisher permission required to reproduce. All rights reserved.

Quotes on page 258–265, 269–272 by Brian Jones. Copyright 2011 by Brian Jones, *Hell is Real (But I Hate to Admit It)* Published by David C. Cook. Publisher permission required to reproduce. All rights reserved.

Page design and layout: Crosslin Creative

Infographics:

"What the Bible Says About Heaven" © 2013 by TheBiblePeople.com. Used by permission.
"The New Jerusalem" taken from *The QuickView Bible* © 2012 by Zondervan. Used by permission.
"What the Bible Says About Hell" © 2013 by TheBiblePeople.com. Used by permission.
"Consequences of the Fall and the Hope of Heaven" © 2013 by TheBiblePeople.com. Used by permission.

Classic Art (Public Domain):

Heaven

Jan Van Eyck; *The Adoration of the Lamb* (detail); 1432
Gustave Dore; *The Empyrean*, from *The Divine Comedy*; 1857–1868
Hans Memling; *The Last Judgment* (detail); 1467–1471
Francesco Botticini; *Assumption of the Virgin*; c. 1475
J. Augustus Knapp; *Ceres Pleading Before Hades for the Liberation of Persephone*; early 20th c.

Hell

Unknown Artist; *The Punishment of the Damned*; 19th c.
Unknown Artist; *A Soul Tormented in Hell* (detail), from *The Book of the Seven Mortal Sins*; 15th c.
William Blake; *The Thieves and Serpents*, from *The Divine Comedy*; 1827
The Limbourg Brothers; *Tundal's Hell*, from *Tres Riches Heures*; c. 1416
Dieric Bouts; *Descent into Hell* (detail); c. 1468

ISBN: 9781401680251

Printed in the United States of America

14 15 16 17 18 19 RRD 6 5 4 3 2 1

▶| CONTENTS

Part Two: Hell 147

ACKNOWLEDGMENTS

Thanks to a great team who helped me wade through lots of books and research on this topic. I am fully aware this book wouldn't exist without any of you. Special thanks go to: Neil Heater for helping me find and get through all the research; Karen Engle for your always cheerful help; Melissa Peitsch for your ability to organize and keep me sane; Teresanne Russell for creating the new infographics for this book; Caleb Hudson and our friends at Dover for helping find the best images to include; Mary Larsen, Robin Merrill, and Steve Leston for doing a final read and review of the manuscript; and Janay Garrick for helping me develop, work, and rework this manuscript.

Special thanks go to Bob Demoss who came up with the idea for this book. And Alee Anderson of Thomas Nelson: I'm grateful for your editorial skills that helped finalize and perfect the final edition.

Lastly, thanks to my wonderful wife, Amber. Thanks to you and the kids for putting up with the difficult schedule that comes with a life in publishing. You are a blessing to me.

I'm incredibly grateful to you all.

► INTRODUCTION

If you could ask God one question about heaven or hell, what would it be?

I have posed this question to many people, and have heard a variety of responses. Do any of these sound familiar?

- Will heaven be interesting?

- Will we have jobs in heaven?

- Is there sex in heaven?

- Does hell really exist?

- What does an eternity in hell feel like?

- If I'm in heaven, will I see people in hell?

The Bible offers clear answers to some of these questions. Others are a mystery. Where there are no clear answers, there are often hints and insights that allow us to shape informed opinions.

In preparing for this book, I took more than sixty of the questions regarding heaven and hell, and I set out to find the answers. I consulted theologians, pastors, writers, and other great Christian thinkers. And I have collected their insights here for you. It is my prayer that their insights and this book will help you understand heaven and hell a bit better.

Christopher D. Hudson
Facebook.com/Christopher.D.Hudson.books
@ReadEngageApply

PART ONE

HEAVEN

Francesco Botticini;
Assumption of the Virgin;
c. 1475

THE MOMENTS
AFTER DEATH

"No one wants to die. Even people who want to go to heaven don't want to die to get there. And yet death is the destination we all share. No one has ever escaped it. And that is as it should be, because Death is very likely the single best invention of Life. It is Life's change agent. It clears out the old to make way for the new."

—Steve Jobs

"We will never forget them, nor the last time we saw them, this morning, as they prepared for the journey and waved goodbye and 'slipped the surly bonds of earth' to 'touch the face of God.'"

—Ronald Reagan, speech on the *Challenger* disaster

"I'm not afraid of death; I just don't want to be there when it happens."

—Woody Allen

"To the well-organized mind, death is but the next great adventure."

—J. K. Rowling, *Harry Potter and the Sorcerer's Stone*

"It is nothing to die."

—Victor Hugo, *Les Misérables*

"Life is pleasant. Death is peaceful. It's the transition that's troublesome."

—Isaac Asimov

"Some day you will read in the papers that D. L. Moody of East Northfield is dead. Don't you believe a word of it! At that moment I shall be more alive than I am now; I shall have gone up higher, that is all, out of this old clay tenement into a house that is immortal—a body that death cannot touch, that sin cannot taint; a body fashioned like unto His glorious body."

—D. L. Moody

But someone will ask, "How are the dead raised? With what kind of body will they come?" How foolish! What you sow does not come to life unless it dies. When you sow, you do not plant the body that will be, but just a seed, perhaps of wheat or of something else. But God gives it a body as he has determined, and to each kind of seed he gives its own body. Not all flesh is the same: People have one kind of flesh, animals have another, birds another and fish another. There are also heavenly bodies and there are earthly bodies; but the splendor of the heavenly bodies is one kind, and the splendor of the earthly bodies is another. The sun has one kind of splendor, the moon another and the stars another; and star differs from star in splendor.

So will it be with the resurrection of the dead. The body that is sown is perishable, it is raised imperishable; it is sown in dishonor, it is raised in glory; it is sown in weakness, it is raised in power; it is sown a natural body, it is raised a spiritual body.

If there is a natural body, there is also a spiritual body. So it is written: "The first man Adam became a living being"; the last Adam, a life-giving spirit. The spiritual did not come first, but the natural, and after that the spiritual. The first man was of the dust of the earth; the second man is of heaven. As was the earthly man, so are those who are of the earth; and as is the heavenly man, so also are those who are of heaven. And just as we have borne the image of the earthly man, so shall we bear the image of the heavenly man.

I declare to you, brothers and sisters, that flesh and blood cannot inherit the kingdom of God, nor does the perishable inherit the imperishable. Listen, I tell you a mystery: We will not all sleep, but we will all be changed—in a flash, in the twinkling of an eye, at the last trumpet. For the trumpet will sound, the dead will be raised imperishable, and we will be changed. For the perishable must clothe itself with the imperishable, and the mortal with immortality. When the perishable has been clothed with the imperishable, and the mortal with immortality, then the saying that is written will come true: "Death has been swallowed up in victory."

> "Where, O death, is your victory?
> Where, O death, is your sting?"

The sting of death is sin, and the power of sin is the law. But thanks be to God! He gives us the victory through our Lord Jesus Christ.

Therefore, my dear brothers and sisters, stand firm. Let nothing move you. Always give yourselves fully to the work of the Lord, because you know that your labor in the Lord is not in vain.

—1 CORINTHIANS 15:35–58

 ## WHAT HAPPENS RIGHT AFTER DEATH?

And if I go and prepare a place for you, I will come back and take you to be with me that you also may be where I am.

—JOHN 14:3

When you're scared or heading into the unknown, who's the one person you want by your side? For me, that person is my wife. She's been my safe, trustworthy companion for twenty years. I know that she won't let me down or abandon me in my time of need. When we think about facing death and going into the unknown without our loved ones, it's comforting to know that someone more trustworthy than anyone on earth will be there to take our hands.

The Bible speaks of the One who will greet us on the other side of death—Christ himself. Scripture says that he has gone to prepare a place for us and will welcome us into our eternal home.

On this topic, Billy Graham wrote the following:

A young man with an incurable disease was reported to have said, "I don't think I would be afraid to die if I knew what to expect after death." Evidently this young man had not heard of what God has prepared for those who love Him.

The man had within him the fear of death. For the Christian there need be no fear. Christ has taken away the fear of death and has given hope.

Jesus said, "I go to prepare a place for you. And if I go . . . I will come again and receive you to Myself" (John 14:2-3). And that place, according to the Apostle Paul, is a "far better" place. Paul wrote, "having a desire to depart and be with Christ, which is far better" (Philippians 1:23).

The grave is not the end. For those who don't know Christ, death is a calamity—eternity in Hell. For the Christian, death holds a glorious hope—the hope of Heaven. But you ask, "What kind of place is Heaven, and how can I go there?"

First, Heaven is home. The Bible takes the word home, with all of its tender associations and with all of its sacred memories, applies it to the hereafter and tells us that Heaven is home.

Just before Christ went to the cross, He gathered His disciples in the upper room and talked about a home. He said: "In my Father's house are many mansions" (John 14:2). When Jesus spoke of Heaven as "My Father's house," He was referring to it as home. The Father's house is always home.

The Bible teaches that you have a soul. Your soul has certain attributes, such as conscience, memory, intelligence and consciousness. Your soul is the real "you." Your body soon goes to the grave, but your soul lives on. The Bible teaches that the moment Christians die they go immediately into the presence of Christ (2 Corinthians 5:6-8). We go home to a place the Bible calls Heaven.

The body is the house in which the soul resides temporarily. The soul is never completely satisfied and happy here, because the soul is not home yet. The true home of the soul is with Christ.

Second, Heaven is a *permanent* home. One of the unfortunate facts about the houses people build for themselves is that they are not permanent. Houses do not last forever. . . .

During Christ's ministry on earth, He had no home. He once said, "Foxes have holes and birds of the air have nests, but the Son of Man has nowhere to lay His head" (Matthew 8:20).

Those who for Christ's sake had given up houses and lands and loved ones knew little of home life or home joys. It was as if Jesus had said to them: "We have no lasting home here on earth, but my Father's house is a home where we will be together for all eternity."

Amid all the changes that sooner or later will come to break up the earthly home, we have the promise of a home where Christ's followers will remain forever. . . .

Our permanent home is not here on earth. Our permanent home is Heaven. Sometimes when things do not go right down here, we get homesick for Heaven. Many times in the midst of the sin, suffering and sorrow of this life, there is a tug at our soul. That is homesickness coupled with anticipation.

For the Christian, death holds a glorious hope—the hope of Heaven.

You may be lying on a hospital bed today, you may be suffering from terrible disease or financial loss or bereavement, and there is a tug in your heart. You are longing for home. You are longing for Heaven.

Third, the Bible teaches that Heaven is a beautiful home. Almost all of us like to beautify our homes. There is something wrong with the home where there are no flowers in the yard and no pictures on the walls, where no effort at all has been put forth to make the home attractive.

Very few people have their homes as beautiful as they would like to have them, but the Bible teaches that Heaven will be a glorious and beautiful place. Heaven could not help but be so, because God is a God of beauty. . . .

All of us who know Christ personally are not afraid to die. Death is not the "grim reaper" to Christians. For us it is not the last great enemy. Death to the Christian is "going home."[1]

Jesus says that he will never leave us or forsake us, so why wouldn't he be there for us when we pass from death to life? Surely, we can trust that he will help us let go of this life and our loved ones on earth. Jesus promises to be there for us immediately after death to comfort and guide us into the wonders he has in store for us.

FOR FURTHER THOUGHT

How might Jesus take away some of the fears that you have about death and dying?

---

1. Excerpts taken from "Heaven is Real" by Billy Graham, March 2012 *Decision* magazine, ©1996 Billy Graham Evangelistic Association. All rights reserved.

IS DEATH THE DOORWAY TO HEAVEN?

> By faith Enoch was taken from this life, so that he did not experience death: "He could not be found, because God had taken him away." For before he was taken, he was commended as one who pleased God.
>
> **—HEBREWS 11:5**

My Greek professor at Wheaton College used to open class with devotions and prayer. His insights were so heartfelt—and so profound—that those few minutes became the highlight of my day. I remember him speaking quite often of a faithful man named Enoch (Heb. 11:5). The Greek word that Scripture uses to describe Enoch's transition from this life to the next means "translation." It implies movement from death to spiritual life. "Death isn't something to be feared," my professor would say. "It's just translation from one life to the next, like a simple word translation from one language to another." The essence of who we are is unchanged; just the language, or expression, has changed. Have you ever thought of death in that way?

If that translation process, or passing from one life to the next, seems frightening or unsettling, it's only because of our limited perspective of our journey. We cling to this life—with all its frailties, imperfections, pain, and sorrow—because it's all we know. Yet Scripture makes it clear that what awaits us in God's presence is beyond even our fondest imagination.

Recently, I recounted this a little more deeply on my blog:

One of Jesus' final statements on the cross—"Father, into your hands I commit my spirit" (Luke 23:46)—offers comfort and assurance to all who follow him. The moment we pass from this life, we will find ourselves in the hands of our loving heavenly Father. We have no reason to fear that passage—and every reason to look forward to it.

A friend of mine tells the story of traveling home for Christmas break during his freshman year at Taylor University. At the time, first-semester freshmen weren't allowed to have cars on campus, so my friend had to wait for his parents to make the fifty-mile drive to campus from their home in central Indiana.

By the time they arrived, the campus was nearly deserted. Dire warnings of an approaching "storm of the century" had prompted most students and faculty to accelerate their departures. A campus job and a particularly unfavorable final exam schedule had prevented my friend from doing the same.

He and his parents quickly loaded the car, a 1982 Lincoln Continental, as a nasty mix of snow and ice began to fall. They made their way with some difficulty through the tiny towns and back roads that surrounded the campus until they reached Highway 13, the two-lane road they would follow the remaining thirty-five miles home.

And that's when the excitement *really* began.

Visibility dropped from a mile to half a mile to one-tenth of a mile, until it descended into near whiteout conditions. The temperature plummeted. A radio newscaster warned of the dangers of the below-zero windchill factor and strongly advised all listeners to stay in their houses.

Unfortunately, staying put was no longer an option for the family, who were ever-so-slowly working their way

> The moment we pass from this life, we will find ourselves in the hands of our loving heavenly Father.

south on Highway 13. With no snowplows in sight and a windshield that was freezing over faster than the defrost blower could warm it, improvisation became a necessity. In certain spots, my friend, who was riding shotgun, and his father, who was driving, were forced to open their doors and peer down at the ground in order to make sure they were still on the road. My friend's mother, meanwhile, sent up white-knuckled prayers from the backseat.

The Lincoln steadily inched its way along as the tension inside the car mounted. One ill-advised turn of the wheel, one momentary loss of tire traction, could have been disastrous. That particular stretch of road was notoriously desolate. What's more, the family had yet to see another car on Highway 13. And in those days before cell phones, there would have been no way to call for help if they had found themselves stranded.

So they pressed on, mile after agonizing mile, praying and sweating it out every inch of the way.

Some six hours after they had started their journey home, they spotted a welcome sight: the red and blue flashing lights of two police cars from their hometown parked perpendicularly across the northbound lane of Highway 13. Just beyond them was a large "Road Closed" sign in the middle of the highway.

The family pulled alongside the stunned police officers, who informed them that Highway 13 had been shut down for hours in both directions due to impassable road conditions.

Imagine the joy, relief, and thankfulness those family members felt when they finally walked in the door of their home—the destination they had envisioned for so long. Imagine how good it must have been to reunite with their loved ones there.

Perhaps that's just a very small taste of what it will be like to pass through heaven's doorway.[2]

A couple of years ago, that beloved Greek professor was translated from this world to the next. I was sad to see my mentor leave this earth, but I look forward to rejoining him as my own life is translated from a faulty earthly language to a perfect heavenly tongue.

FOR FURTHER THOUGHT

How does thinking of death as a transition—or translation—from this life to the next change your perspective?

---

2. Adapted from my blog: www.ReadEngageApply.com. Used by permission.

HOW WILL MY RESURRECTED BODY BE DIFFERENT FROM MY CURRENT BODY?

> But our citizenship is in heaven. And we eagerly await a Savior from there, the Lord Jesus Christ, who, by the power that enables him to bring everything under his control, will transform our lowly bodies so that they will be like his glorious body.
>
> **—PHILIPPIANS 3:20–21**

Celebrities seem to be in constant pursuit of the perfect body. New noses, breasts, and chins abound in Hollywood. While it's easy to snicker at the constant cosmetic work, would we give in to the same temptation if we had all their money and our livelihood depended on looking attractive and youthful? Besides, if given the chance, who wouldn't trade in a broken-down body for a better model that would never get sick, diseased, wrinkled, or overweight? Is that what our heavenly bodies will be like? Will they be perfected versions of our current bodies or something entirely new?

Author and Christian leader Randy Alcorn wrote on this topic in his book *Heaven*:

> The empty tomb is the ultimate proof that Christ's resurrection body was the same body that died on the cross. If

resurrection meant the creation of a new body, Christ's original body would have remained in the tomb. When Jesus said to his disciples after his resurrection, "It is I myself," he was emphasizing to them that he was the same person—in spirit *and* body—who had gone to the cross (Luke 24:39). His disciples saw the marks of his crucifixion, unmistakable evidence that this was the same body.

Jesus said, "Destroy this temple, and I will raise it again in three days" (John 2:19). John clarifies that "the temple he had spoken of was his body" (v. 21). The body that rose is the body that was destroyed. Hence, Hank Hanegraaff says, "There is a one-to-one correspondence between the body of Christ that died and the body that rose."[3]

In its historic crystallization of orthodox doctrine, the Westminster *Larger Catechism* (1647) states, "The self-same bodies of the dead which were laid in the grave, being then again united to their souls forever, shall be raised up by the power of Christ."[4] The Westminster Confession, one of the great creeds of the Christian faith, says, "All the dead shall be raised up, with the self-same bodies, and none other."[5] "Self-same bodies" affirms the doctrine of continuity through resurrection.

This, then, is the most basic truth about our resurrected bodies: They are the same bodies God created for us, but they will be raised to greater perfection than we've ever known. We don't know everything about them, of course, but *we do*

---

3. Hank Hanegraaff, *Resurrection* (Nashville: Word, 2000), 68–69.

4. Peter Toon, *Longing for Heaven: A Devotional Look at the Life after Death* (New York: Macmillan, 1986), 141.

5. *The Westminster Confession of Faith*, Chap. XXXII, "Of the State of Men after Death, and of the Resurrection of the Dead," http://www.pcanet.org/general/cof_chapxxxi-xxxiii.htm.

know a great deal. Scripture does not leave us in the dark about our resurrection bodies.

Because we each have a physical body, we already have the single best reference point for envisioning a *new* body. It's like the new upgrade of my word processing software. When I heard there was an upgrade available, I didn't say, "I have no idea what it will be like." I knew that for the most part it would be like the old program, only better. Sure, it has some new features that I didn't expect, and I'm glad for them. But I certainly recognize it as the same program I've used for a decade.

Likewise, when we receive our resurrected bodies, we'll no doubt have some welcome surprises—maybe even some new features (though no glitches or programming errors)— but we'll certainly recognize our new bodies as being *ours.* God has given us working models to guide our imagination about what our new bodies will be like on the New Earth.[6]

In another writing, Alcorn added:

Scripture portrays resurrection as involving both funda-mental continuity and significant dissimilarity. We dare not minimize the dissimilarities—for our glorification will certainly involve a dramatic and marvelous transformation. But, in my experience, the great majority of Christians have underemphasized continuity. They end up thinking of our transformed selves as no longer being ourselves, and the transformed Earth as no longer being the earth. In some cases, they view the glorified Christ as no longer being the same Jesus who walked the earth—a belief that early Chris-tians recognized as heresy.

---

6. Randy Alcorn, *Heaven* (Wheaton, IL: Tyndale House Publishers, 2004), 113–14.

Many of us look forward to Heaven more now than we did when our bodies functioned well. Joni Eareckson Tada says it well: "Somewhere in my broken, paralyzed body is the seed of what I shall become. The paralysis makes what I am to become all the more grand when you contrast atrophied, useless legs against splendorous resurrected legs. I'm convinced that if there are mirrors in heaven (and why not?), the image I'll see will be unmistakably 'Joni,' although a much better, brighter Joni."[7]

Inside your body, even if it is failing, is the blueprint for your resurrection body. You may not be satisfied with your current body or mind—but you'll be thrilled with your resurrection upgrades. With them you'll be better able to serve and glorify God and enjoy an eternity of wonders he has prepared for you.[8]

Plastic surgeons and doctors will need new careers in the new heaven because God will give each of us a wonderfully new and perfected body. I'm looking forward to my heavenly body without these scars, aches, unhealthy weight gains, and weaknesses. How about you?

FOR FURTHER THOUGHT

What aspect of your resurrected body are you looking forward to the most?

---

7. Joni Eareckson Tada, *Heaven: Your Real Home* (Grand Rapids: Zondervan, 1995), 39.

8. Randy Alcorn, "What Will Our Glorified Bodies Be Like?" Kindle edition.

WHAT WILL JESUS HAVE FOR ME IN HEAVEN?

> When the Chief Shepherd appears, you will receive the crown of glory that will never fade away.
>
> —1 PETER 5:4

Even people who are great at so many things and receive tons of praise and recognition on earth cannot possibly be good at everything, right? Even the most popular, beautiful, and wealthy among us know what it's like to be forgotten, to be passed over. To be unseen is one of the greatest disappointments on earth. When people feel unseen, they feel unloved. In heaven, will we finally know we are seen and loved by Jesus? Will he give each one of us the recognition and the gaze that we have so longed for on earth?

When certain key passages of Scripture are pieced together, we get a picture of a Savior who will lavish attention on us for eternity. We may not have the ability to understand everything that heaven holds for us, but we can draw up a primer of sorts— an itinerary of experiences to look forward to. I once pulled together a list of ten of the promises God has made regarding heaven. Here is the list:

1. We will get our first glimpse of our Savior.

Stephen was being stoned to death when he caught his first glimpse. Despite his dire earthly circumstances, he exclaimed with wonder and awe, "Look! I see heaven open and the Son of Man standing at the right hand of God" (Acts 7:56). That same sense of wonder and awe awaits us.

2. We will be escorted to our heavenly destination by angels.

In the middle of his story about an encounter between a rich man and a beggar named Lazarus, Jesus offered this tantalizing description: "The time came when the beggar died and the angels carried him to Abraham's side" (Luke 16:22). When Jesus' followers go to heaven, they go in style.

3. We will enjoy a private reception with Jesus.

As Stephen felt his life slipping away, he made one simple yet profound request: "Lord Jesus, receive my spirit" (Acts 7:59). Is it a stretch to suggest that Jesus honored his request—or that the Lord personally welcomes *all* his faithful servants into eternity?

4. We will break free of the curse once and for all.

Revelation 22:3 reveals that the curse that God placed on his creation as a result of Adam and Eve's sin in the Garden of Eden will be lifted in heaven. For the first time, we will be able to experience God's creation as he intended.

5. We will discover what it is like not to suffer.

The promise of Revelation 21:4 is enough to bring tears to the eyes of anyone who has endured pain, suffering, depression, hardship, loss, or grief. " '[God] will wipe every tear from their eyes. There will be no more death' or mourning or crying or pain, for the old order of things has passed away."

6. We will experience the joy of the Lord.

The words the faithful servant heard in Matthew 25:21 will be the same words we hear when we are welcomed into heaven: "Well done, good and faithful servant! You have been faithful with a few things; I will put you in charge of many things. Come and share your master's happiness!"

7. We will be welcomed into the presence of God.

In the Old Testament, God's presence was accessible only to a select few, at very specific times, and under extremely restrictive conditions. That will not be the case in heaven. "Look! God's dwelling place is now among the people, and he will dwell with them. They will be his people, and God himself will be with them and be their God" (Revelation 21:3).

8. We will serve him.

"[God's] servants will serve him" (Revelation 22:3). If that prospect seems less than appealing, consider this: we were created to serve him. In heaven, we will know what it is like to find true fulfillment and soul-deep satisfaction in our work.

9. We will become like Christ.

The apostle John explained it this way: "Dear friends, now we are children of God, and what we will be has not yet been made known. But we know that when

Everything that is wrong in this world will be made right in heaven.

Christ appears, we shall be like him, for we shall see him as he is" (1 John 3:2).

10. We will spend eternity with our Creator and our Savior.

At the heart of the most-quoted verse in all Scripture is the guarantee that our fellowship will never end: "For God so loved the world that he gave his one and only Son, that whoever believes in him shall not perish but have eternal life" (John 3:16).[9]

Everything that is wrong in this world will be made right in heaven. Rather than dread the end of our time in this world, we can eagerly anticipate a place where the things that *really* matter will be the *only* things that matter.

In heaven we won't obsess with our brains, beauty, or bank accounts. We will enjoy our time with God and finally know what it is like to live a pain-free, perfect existence. That's a final chapter I'm really looking forward to.

FOR FURTHER THOUGHT

Which of the ten promises above are you looking forward to most?

---

9. Adapted from my blog: www.ReadEngageApply.com. Used by permission.

WHAT IS OUR **HEAVENLY "INHERITANCE"?**

> Those who are victorious will inherit all this, and I will be their God and they will be my children.
>
> **—REVELATION 21:7**

I can't imagine what it would be like to have no concerns about money, can you? Unfortunately, by the time we're adults, most Americans have learned how to abuse a credit card. Debt soon follows along with the stress of financial worries. But there are things in our lives worth far more than cars, houses, and vacations, aren't there? If we love a God who owns "the cattle on a thousand hills" and the entire earth, and we are his sons and daughters, then what will our future inheritance be?

Pastor and author Dave Earley wrote this in *The 21 Most Amazing Truths About Heaven*:

> According to *Forbes* magazine, the richest person on Earth is Bill Gates, the founder of Microsoft. His net worth is fifty billion dollars—that is a five plus ten zeroes! Gates is a self-made man who dropped out of college to start a computer company thirty years ago. If he were to divide his wealth among his three children, they would each be among the richest people on Earth.[10]
>
> Sam Walton began as a JCPenney clerk but opened his first discount store in Rogers, Arkansas, in 1962. His little

---

10. Luisa Kroll and Allison Fass, ed. "The World's Billionaires" (March 9, 2006), http://www.forbes.com/billionaires.

store, Wal-Mart, has become the world's largest retailer, with more than 5,100 stores serving 138 million customers per week. At his death in 1992, each of his four children received over five billion dollars. They are now worth over three times that amount.[11]

The Bible is very clear that we are the heirs of God. In Heaven we have an inheritance waiting for us. We will be the heirs of God Himself, who has promised,

> He who overcomes will inherit all this, and I will be his God and he will be my son. Revelation 21:7
>
> Now if we are children, then we are heirs—heirs of God and co-heirs with Christ. Romans 8:17
>
> Praise be to the God and Father of our Lord Jesus Christ! In his great mercy he has given us new birth into a living hope through the resurrection of Jesus Christ from the dead, and into an inheritance that can never perish, spoil, or fade—kept in heaven for you. 1 Peter 1:3–4

Our inheritance could easily dwarf anything anyone on Earth has ever received. How much will we inherit in Heaven? The answer is easy. We will inherit exactly the amount that is best for us and exactly the amount we deserve. If we were generous in making eternal investments in Heaven, God will be generous in giving us our inheritance in Heaven (Matthew 6:19–21).

According to *Forbes*, Updown Court, Windlesham, England, is currently the most expensive residence on the market in the world with an asking price of $122 million. The brand-new property is totally over the top, with 103 rooms, five swimming pools, and 24-carat gold leafing on

---

11. "Freeze and Squeeze," http://gift-estate.com/article/Freeze.htm.

the study's mosaic floor. There's a squash court, bowling alley, tennis court, 50-seat screening room, heated marble driveway, and helipad. All eight of your limousines will fit in the underground garage. The neighbors include the Queen of England at Windsor Castle.[12]

Jesus promised us special dwellings connected to the Father's house.

> In My Father's house are many dwelling places; if it were not so, I would have told you; for I go to prepare a place for you. John 14:2 NASB

We don't know much more about these residences, but we can be sure that they will be exactly the best size, style, shape, and location for us. In our heavenly homes, we will enjoy being neighbors with the King—that is King Jesus, the King of kings and the Lord of lords! . . .

Apart from God being there, one of the greatest points about Heaven is its amazing availability to all who truly want in. Granted, I realize that some people don't want 100 percent of God 100 percent of the time. Some people have no stomach for good, clean fun. Some are repulsed by the thought of endless morning, perpetual beauty, and never-ending spring. Some hate worship, mock truth, and discount or deny Jesus. The bottom line is they simply don't want to be in Heaven.

Don't worry.

God won't make them go. Heaven is only available to those who really *want* to be there. It is *free* to those who will receive the free gift of the water of life, by expressed faith in Jesus Christ the Lord.

---

12. Sara Clemence, "The Most Expensive Homes in the World," http://www.forbes. com/2005/07/26/cx_sc_0729home_eu.html?thisSpeed=6000.

The new Heaven will be a God-filled, pleasure-packed, new, thirst-quenching inheritance available to all who truly want to be there. The big question for us to ask ourselves is this: Do we love God enough to want to spend eternity with Him? If so, we can. You can come to Him right now in prayer. Tell Him that you want to spend eternity with Him. Tell Him you want to drink deeply of the free gift of the water of life. If you really mean it, reservations will be made for you in Heaven.[13]

I have a feeling that all the "stuff" we care about on earth just won't matter when we're in God's presence. We won't care how big our houses are or how many fun cars we have in the driveway. We'll have an inheritance that cannot compare to anything on this earth: the treasures of our heavenly King and the beauty of his kingdom.

FOR FURTHER THOUGHT

The psalmist wrote, "Turn my eyes away from worthless things; preserve my life according to your word" (Ps. 119:37). Are there areas in which God wants to shift your focus?

---

13. Dave Earley, *The 21 Most Amazing Truths About Heaven* (Uhrichsville, OH: Barbour Publishing, 2006), 132–135.

WILL I BE SMARTER IN HEAVEN?

For now we see only a reflection as in a mirror; then we shall see face to face. Now I know in part; then I shall know fully, even as I am fully known.

—1 CORINTHIANS 13:12

Sir Francis Bacon said, "Knowledge is power."[14] Where people are educated, societies often flourish. Western cultures place a high value on education and gaining knowledge, but what if there is a knowledge that is better than any PhD program or college degree? What if there's a type of knowledge or wisdom that surpasses all human understanding?

Dave Earley had this to say on the topic:

Heaven is a mind-expanding experience.

We will know much more in Heaven than we do now, but we will not know everything. Only God is infinite; therefore, only God knows everything. We will know more fully, but not exhaustively.

We don't *need* to know everything there is to know. I doubt that I'll *need* to know how many grains of salt are in my salt shaker, or the total number of words ever printed on every book, typewriter, and computer screen in history, or even the batting average of Mickey Mantle in 1961. (It's .317, by the way.)

---

14. http://www.quotationspage.com/quote/2060.html.

There are also many things I don't think I will ever *want* to know. I don't wish to know how many earthworms have ever lived. I have no desire to know the intricate details of the life of maggots. There are many things I just don't want to know.

While it is true we won't know everything in Heaven, we will know much more, much more fully, and much more accurately than we do now. One scholar writes,

> 1 Corinthians 13:12 . . . rightly translated, simply says that we will know in a fuller or more intensive way, "even as we have been known," that is without error or misconceptions in our knowledge.[15]

Many life issues that have always been murky will become crystal clear in the golden light of Heaven. Pieces of the puzzle will come together. Confusing matters will make sense.

Learning and growing are what keep life from becoming mundane. Contrary to popular opinion, life in Heaven will be anything but mundane. One reason Heaven will be such a vibrant place is because we will continue to learn in Heaven. We will have the time and opportunity to be taught more than we could ever imagine on Earth.

Among other things, we will know more about God, the Bible, the mystery of salvation, the complexities of the universe, the history of the world, and more about ourselves than we could possibly ever know now. In Heaven our capacity for knowing and understanding will be greatly expanded. Also, our opportunity for knowing and understanding will be wildly enhanced. We will have the greatest guides imaginable. . . .

---

15. Wayne Grudem, *Systematic Theology: An Introduction to Biblical Doctrine* (Grand Rapids: Zondervan, 1994), endnote on 1162.

In heaven, we will be supplied with God's wisdom about our lives.

In Heaven we will have the opportunity to learn skills that we did not have the time or ability to acquire on earth. I hope to draw and paint the pictures I have mentally recorded during my lifetime. I also anticipate painting heavenly sights that can only be imagined on Earth. I hope to learn to play the piano and the guitar really well. I want to understand the nuances of music well enough to write a symphony. I want to write songs. Why not? I will have access to wonderful teachers and all of eternity to practice.

In Heaven we will not only have more information, we'll have a better context for that information. We'll see facts through the 20/20 vision of eternity. We'll see the events of life as they are reflected in the eyes of the Master, especially the events of our lives.

The point of Mitch Albom's best-selling fictional story *The Five People You Meet in Heaven* is that the first five people you meet in Heaven will illuminate the unseen or misunderstood connections of our earthly lives.

> People think of heaven as a paradise garden, a place where they float on clouds and laze in rivers and mountains. But scenery without solace is meaningless. This is the greatest gift God can give you: to understand what happened in your life. To have it explained. It is the peace you have been searching for.[16]

---

16. Mitch Albom, *The Five People You Meet in Heaven* (New York: Hyperion, 2003), 35.

>While I don't fully accept Albom's view of Heaven, I do think he is right about one thing. From the vantage point of Heaven, we will accurately be able to understand our lives and the meaning of the events of our lives. We will finally have answers to the "why?" questions that taint our joy and plague our minds down here on Earth. Missing pieces of the puzzle will be supplied.
>
>Don't be frustrated by all you can't and don't understand now. In Heaven you will be continually learning and growing as a person. The day is coming when you will know and understand much more than you ever imagined possible. All of the various events of your life will finally make sense.[17]

Because our understanding on earth is always limited and partial, so much of our earthly lives involve trust, risk, and faith. In heaven, we will be supplied with God's wisdom about our lives. That's the type of "smarts" I'm looking forward to gaining in heaven.

FOR FURTHER THOUGHT

What is one life event that you can't wait to understand more fully?

17. Dave Earley, *The 21 Most Amazing Truths About Heaven* (Uhrichsville, OH: Barbour Publishing, 2006), 155–157, 159–160.

LIFE IN HEAVEN

Jan Van Eyck;
The Adoration of the Lamb (detail);
1432

"Our life of poverty is as necessary as the work itself. Only in heaven will we see how much we owe to the poor for helping us to love God better because of them."

—Mother Teresa

"Listen to God with a broken heart. He is not only the doctor who mends it, but also the father who wipes away the tears."

—Criss Jami

"Death is no more than passing from one room into another. But there's a difference for me, you know. Because in that other room I shall be able to see."

—Helen Keller

"Fear not death for the sooner we die, the longer we shall be immortal."

—Benjamin Franklin

"Death ends a life, not a relationship."

—Mitch Albom, *Tuesdays with Morrie*

"To enter heaven is to become more human than you ever succeeded in being on earth; to enter hell is to be banished from humanity."

—C. S. Lewis, *The Problem of Pain*

"If you are not allowed to laugh in heaven,
then I don't want to go there."
—Martin Luther

Then I looked and heard the voice of many angels, numbering thousands upon thousands, and ten thousand times ten thousand. They encircled the throne and the living creatures and the elders. In a loud voice they were saying:

"Worthy is the Lamb, who was slain,
to receive power and wealth and wisdom and
strength
and honor and glory and praise!"

Then I heard every creature in heaven and on earth and under the earth and on the sea, and all that is in them, saying:

"To him who sits on the throne and to the Lamb
be praise and honor and glory and power,
for ever and ever!"

The four living creatures said, "Amen," and the elders fell down and worshiped.

—REVELATION 5:11–14

WILL WE HAVE PHYSICAL BODIES IN HEAVEN?

> And if the Spirit of him who raised Jesus from the dead is living in you, he who raised Christ from the dead will also give life to your mortal bodies because of his Spirit who lives in you.
> **—ROMANS 8:11**

Do you like your physical body? Unfortunately, many of us would say, "No, thank you," and we would be happy to ditch them in heaven. But is that likely to happen? Will we have physical bodies in the new heaven and new earth? Or will we leave our bodies in the grave and become merely spirits? Randy Alcorn, director of Eternal Perspective Ministries, answers these questions:

> The major Christian creeds state, "I believe in the resurrection of the body." But I have found in many conversations that Christians tend to spiritualize the resurrection of the dead, effectively denying it.[18] They don't reject it as a doctrine, but they deny its essential *meaning*: a permanent return to a physical existence in a physical universe.
>
> Of Americans who believe in a resurrection of the dead, two-thirds believe they will not have bodies after the

---

18. For Paul's exposition of the resurrection of the dead, see 1 Corinthians 15:12–58.

resurrection.[19] But this is self-contradictory. A non-physical resurrection is like a sunless sunrise. There's no such thing. Resurrection *means* that we will have bodies. If we didn't have bodies, we wouldn't be resurrected!

The biblical doctrine of the resurrection of the dead begins with the human body but extends far beyond it. R. A. Torrey writes, "We will not be disembodied spirits in the world to come, but redeemed spirits, in redeemed bodies, in a redeemed universe."[20] If we don't get it right on the resurrection of the body, we'll get nothing else right. It's therefore critical that we not merely affirm the resurrection of the dead as a point of doctrine but that we *understand* the meaning of the resurrection we affirm.

Genesis 2:7 says, "The Lord God formed the man from the dust of the ground and breathed into his nostrils the breath of life, and the man became a living being." The Hebrew word for "living being" is *nephesh*, often translated "soul." The point at which Adam became *nephesh* is when God joined his body (dust) and spirit (breath) together. Adam was not a living human being until he had both material (physical) and immaterial (spiritual) components. Thus, the essence of humanity is not just spirit, but *spirit joined with body*. Your body does not merely house the real you—it is as much a part of who you are as your spirit is.

If this idea seems wrong to us, it's because we have been deeply influenced by Christoplatonism. From a christoplatonic perspective, our souls merely occupy our bodies, like a hermit crab inhabits a seashell, and our souls could naturally—or even ideally—live in a disembodied state.

---

19. *Time* (March 24, 1997): 75, quoted in Paul Marshall with Lela Gilbert, *Heaven Is Not My Home: Learning to Live in God's Creation* (Nashville: Word, 1998), 234.

20. R. A. Torrey, *Heaven or Hell* (New Kensington, PA: Whitaker House, 1985), 68–69.

It's no coincidence that the apostle Paul's detailed defense of the physical resurrection of the dead was written to the church at Corinth. More than any other New Testament Christians, the Corinthian believers were immersed in the Greek philosophies of Platonism and dualism, which perceived a dichotomy between the spiritual and the physical. The biblical view of human nature, however, is radically different. Scripture indicates that God designed our bodies to be an integral part of our total being. Our physical bodies are an essential aspect of who we are, not just shells for our spirits to inhabit.

Death is an abnormal condition because it tears apart what God created and joined together. God intended for our bodies to last as long as our souls. Those who believe in Platonism or in preexistent spirits see a disembodied soul as natural and even desirable. The Bible sees it as unnatural and undesirable. We are unified beings. That's why the bodily resurrection of the dead is so vital. And that's why Job rejoiced that *in his flesh he would see God* (Job 19:26).

When God sent Jesus to die, it was for our bodies as well as our spirits. He came to redeem not just "the breath of life" (spirit) but also "the dust of the ground" (body). When we die, it isn't that our real self goes to the intermediate Heaven and our fake self goes to the grave; it's that part of us goes to the intermediate Heaven and part goes to the grave to await our bodily resurrection. We will never be all that God intended for us to be until body and spirit are again joined in resurrection. (If we do have physical forms in the intermediate state, clearly they will not be our original or ultimate bodies.)[21]

---

21. Randy Alcorn, *Heaven* (Wheaton, IL: Tyndale House Publishers, 2004), 110–11.

We need both our spirits and our bodies to become the beautiful creations that God intended us to be. Without one or the other, we would not be fully human. So we can look forward to the "reunion" of our bodies, in their perfected states, with our souls in heaven. If that's difficult to imagine, it's because we haven't lived with perfect bodies or perfect souls, nor have we experienced perfect unity between the two. It will come, though. And when it does, it will be amazing.

FOR FURTHER THOUGHT

Can you imagine what it will be like to have a new body in the new creation?

WILL THERE BE SEX IN HEAVEN?

> You make known to me the path of life;
>   you will fill me with joy in your
>   presence,
>   with eternal pleasures at your right
>   hand.

—PSALM 16:11

When I asked my Facebook community what questions they would ask God about heaven, I wasn't surprised when the conversation turned to sex. It's one thing that a lot of us can't imagine doing without in heaven. As one of our greatest earthly pleasures, would God ban it from heaven? But didn't Jesus say there would be no marriage in heaven? And if there's no marriage, does that also mean no sex? Is the intimacy and pleasure that we experience during sex merely a preview of the greatest joy we will experience in heaven?

Who better than C. S. Lewis to discuss something so deep and personal? Here, Christian professor Wayne Martindale wrestles with some of Lewis's writings on the subject:

> There are lots of "no more's" in Heaven that we happily embrace: "no more tears," "no more sorrow," "no more death." But at least one of the "no more's" we might like to have been consulted about, namely, sex. Jesus said, speaking of saved people, that "in the resurrection they neither marry nor are given in marriage, but are like angels in heaven."[22] I remember reading that and thinking, *Poor angels—poor me!* Or so I thought. As a teenager, I used to pray that Jesus would not come again until I had had my honeymoon. I didn't want to leave earth before enjoying God's great gift of sexuality. It was a mostly silly prayer, but it was nonetheless sincere, and I suspect that among those who grew up with Bible training, I was not alone.
>
> Why do we have this fear? It is because we think, perhaps subconsciously, that Heaven will mean deprivation. What, no sex? What will people do for fun? Isn't that implied in our thinking? Of course it is. But in truth, we will be uninterested in sexuality in Heaven not because it is "atrophied" but because it is "engulfed."[23]

---

22. Matthew 22:30.

23. C. S. Lewis, *Perelandra* (New York: Macmillan, 1965), 3:32–33. Here Lewis's narrator says, "In Ransom's opinion, the present functions and appetites of the body would disappear, not because they were atrophied, but because they were, as he said, 'engulfed.'"

To explain this phenomenon, Lewis uses the apt analogy of a small boy who loves chocolates. Upon being told that "the sexual act is the highest bodily pleasure," the boy immediately asks

> whether you [eat] chocolates at the same time. On receiving the answer "No," he might regard absence of chocolates as the chief characteristic of sexuality. In vain would you tell him that the reason why lovers in their carnal raptures don't bother about chocolates is that they have something better to think of. The boy knows chocolate: he does not know the positive thing that excludes it. We are in the same position. We know the sexual life; we do not know, except in glimpses, the other thing which, in Heaven, will leave no room for it. Hence where fullness [sic] awaits us we anticipate fasting.[24]

What really awaits us is a fulfillment of our sexuality that is as unimaginable to us as sexuality itself is to a child not yet through puberty. But is that prepubescent child asexual? No. The sexuality is there, shaping crucial aspects of personality and self. It is just not yet in full bloom. I believe that death will be a kind of spiritual puberty for us and that Heaven will fulfill desires we don't even know about yet, but which are very much there in *potentia*, working even now in our personalities and our sanctification. . . .

Lewis believes that God is beyond time and space: They are his invention and do not contain him; rather, he contains them. But we will likely occupy both time and space in Heaven, and it is possible to think of ourselves as having more than three dimensions of space and more than one

---

24. C. S. Lewis, *Miracles* (New York: Macmillan, 1978), 16:160.

dimension of time.[25] With just one more dimension of time, we would be able to spend an infinite amount of time with every person, all the time.[26] Such intimacy we can't even have with just one person in our single dimension. The usefulness of this idea is mainly in stimulating our imaginations to think of Heaven as *more* than earth, not less: to see Heaven as adding to, not taking away. If there is no marrying in Heaven, it is because even our earthly best relationships are subsumed by Heaven's new relationships, with deeper intimacy unspoiled by sin. No sex? No problem. It is not that sex is taken away, but taken up into something even greater. Once again where we fear fasting, there is really feasting.[27]

Heaven is a place of higher pleasure, communion, and intimacy that we can't imagine here on earth. To focus too much on sex or to be disappointed that it may not exist in heaven shows that our views of heaven and God are simply too low. After all, God is the one who made pleasure and created us to enjoy him and others. So we must wait and trust that other heavenly delights will be revealed.

---

25. Lewis has many intriguing speculations on how we might experience time differently after this earthly life. His creative liberty with the time lapse between earth and Narnia is one. In *Miracles*, he suggests that "time may not always be for us, as it is now, unilinear and irreversible" (16:153); in *Reflections on the Psalms* he hopes we will "finally . . . emerge, if not altogether from time (that might not suit our humanity) at any rate from the tyranny, the unilinear poverty, of time" (15:137–138). Lewis also suggests that time might have something like a variable thickness, implying another dimension or two.

26. Hugh Ross, *Beyond the Cosmos: The Extra-Dimensionality of God* (Colorado Springs: NavPress, 1996), 203.

27. Taken from *Beyond the Shadowlands: C.S. Lewis on Heaven and Hell* by Wayne Martindale, © 2005, pp. 30–32. Used by permission of Crossway, a publishing ministry of Good News Publishers, Wheaton, IL 60187, www.crossway.org.

FOR FURTHER THOUGHT

How might your closest relationship on earth be a preview of the closeness to come in God's presence?

HOW WILL OUR THOUGHTS BE DIFFERENT IN HEAVEN?

For now we see only a reflection as in a mirror; then we shall see face to face. Now I know in part; then I shall know fully, even as I am fully known.

—1 CORINTHIANS 13:12

Think for a moment about what you spend time thinking about each day. The glory of God? The great truths found in Scripture? Maybe some of the time, but probably not very often. If you're like me, then you probably wouldn't want to share some of your darkest thoughts with others. Our minds are full of lies, destructive thought patterns, and selfish dreams. When we receive our new bodies and minds in heaven, how will our thoughts be different from what they are now?

Joni Eareckson Tada, a quadriplegic and advocate for disabled persons worldwide, wrote this about an experience she had teaching a Sunday school class to mentally disabled students:

> I look forward to heaven because I've got a lot invested there. A new body. A new heart free of sin. But I have some other friends who have just as much, if not more, invested.

I encountered these friends in a Sunday school class not along ago. . . .

Everybody wanted to hear about heaven. . . .

As their enthusiasm mounted, I finally blurted, "Hey guys, I may have a new body, but one day you will have . . . new . . . *minds*!" The entire class jumped to their feet and wildly applauded. . . .

By the time Sunday school was over, the class was well on their way to setting their hearts and minds on heavenly glories above. They were looking out the window to see if Jesus was coming back, clapping their hands, and jumping up and down. I thought I had taught them a lesson about heaven, but they had taught me what it meant to "have the mind of Christ."

A new mind!

First Corinthians 13:12 describes it this way: "Now we see but a poor reflection as in a mirror; then we shall see face to face. Now I know in part; then I shall know fully, even as I am fully known." We will have the mind of Christ. No need to worry about feeling dumb or not knowing the answers. "We will know as we are known," and our present knowledge shall increase beyond belief. What's more, the shine of our best thoughts and memories will be made more resplendent as they are magnified through our new mind.

But what about the sad thoughts left over from earth? Isaiah 65:17 says, "Behold, I will create new heavens and a new earth. The former things will not be remembered, nor will they come to mind. But be glad and rejoice forever in what I will create." This, at first, looks like a snafu. Didn't we just read that we will fully know *all* things? Are bad things excluded?

Our ignorance or imperfect thoughts and memories won't be erased so much as eclipsed, like the stars are mitigated by the rising of the sun. Something so dazzling is going to happen in the world's finale that its light will obscure every dark memory. We won't forget so much as have no need nor desire to remember. Bad things will not, as Isaiah observes, come to mind, for they will be blocked out by the brilliance of the knowledge of God.

Only good things will come to mind. Our thought processes will no longer connive; we won't devise nasty words or scheme wicked plans. We won't battle against idle daydreams or lustful fantasies. Rather, our thoughts will be gloriously elevated for "when he appears, *we shall be like him*, for we shall see him as he is" (1 John 3:2).

Think of perfect obedience to the Ten Commandments. Having no other gods before the Lord? Easy, we will be one with Him. I don't know about you, but I would love to tiptoe alongside the ranks of the seraphim and harmonize as they constantly proclaim day and night, "Holy, holy, holy is the Lord God Almighty."

Jealousy? You and I will have nothing but admiration for whomever is selected to sit on the right and left hand of Christ. Keeping the Sabbath? We will have entered God's seventh and final day, the Sabbath-rest of peace and joy for eternity.

Adultery? I will love everyone as perfectly as Christ loves, and I will never be grieved with the thought that I am slighted by those I love or that their love is not fully and fondly returned. I will find in every person that facet of the Lord's loveliness that only he or she

Think of perfect obedience to the Ten Commandments.

can uniquely reflect—I'm going to be in love with a mountain of people, both men and women!

Coveting? We will be joint-heirs with Christ. We'll have everything. Bearing false witness? The father of lies will be dead. The flesh will no longer entice us to lie. Only truth will spring from our heart. Misusing the name of the Lord? Only praise will be on our lips. Never a hurtful thought. Oh, happy day, we shall have the mind of Christ! And with the mind of Christ we shall "know fully."[28]

It will be a relief not to have bad, twisted, and crazy thoughts coming in and out of our minds throughout the day, won't it? It will be a relief to see people how they really are instead of through distorted minds. In heaven, we won't have to battle the lies with the truth anymore. In heaven, we will have the mind of Christ.

FOR FURTHER THOUGHT

What are some thoughts you will gladly leave behind?

28. Joni Eareckson Tada, *Heaven: Your Real Home* (Grand Rapids: Zondervan, 2010), 41–44.

IS THERE TRULY NO MOURNING OR PARTING IN HEAVEN?

> Then the angel showed me the river of the water of life, as clear as crystal, flowing from the throne of God and of the Lamb down the middle of the great street of the city. On each side of the river stood the tree of life, bearing twelve crops of fruit, yielding its fruit every month. And the leaves of the tree are for the healing of the nations.
>
> **—REVELATION 22:1-2**

I have said good-bye to a lot of people in my life, haven't you? Saying good-bye seems to be part of the normal human experience. Some good-byes are due to moving and life circumstances; others are due to illness and death. Regardless of what causes the parting, it's always hard—even if there is a reunion scheduled in the future. I think something that adds to the bittersweetness of saying good-bye is the hope that we might be able to say "hello" to our loved ones in the future.

Dr. Tony Evans, the first African American to graduate with a doctoral degree from Dallas Theological Seminary, is one of my favorite preachers. Here's something he has written about heaven:

I don't think there is a Christian who has ever lived who has read Revelation 21:4 without longing for the day when God "will wipe away every tear from their eyes; and there will no longer be any death; there will no longer be any mourning, or crying, or pain; the first things have passed away."

All of the things that make life on earth hard will be wiped away in heaven. We are talking about a place of perfect, righteous pleasure.

This is possible because God says, "I am making all things new" (v. 5). So whatever we have in heaven, it will never grow old. The newness will never wear off. We will never get bored with the old stuff we have and long for new stuff.

You've heard people get up in the morning and say, "I feel like a new person today." They're expressing the joy of feeling good that particular day. In heaven, that feeling will be an ongoing reality. We will always feel like new people! There will be no pain or death because we will never grow old.

You'll also never have any reason to cry in heaven. Psalm 16:11 says that in the Lord's presence we will experience full joy.

Why aren't we experiencing this fullness of joy and righteous pleasure here on earth? After all, James says, "Every good thing given and every perfect gift is from above, coming down from the Father of lights, with whom there is no variation or shifting shadow" (James 1:17).

Everything good we have in life comes from the hand of God, whether it's health or family or material blessings. The reason we don't always enjoy these things is not because of God, but because of what James calls the "shifting shadow."

This refers to the ups and downs, the ebbs and flows of life. People can cause a shadow to come across our lives. Our own sin often plunges us into darkness. The devil seeks to cause shifting shadows to interrupt life. All of us shift and move while God, like the sun at the center of the solar system, remains the same.

So one moment I'm in the sunlight of God, and I'm smiling. But the next moment I'm crying because life has cast a dark shadow across my path. My circumstances have shifted.

But heaven doesn't have any shadows because there is nothing to create a shadow. Heaven is perfect daylight and perfect joy all the time because God is the Light of heaven. . . .

One reason we know that heaven is a place of perfect life is that there will be no pain or sorrow or death there. Perfect life certainly demands the absence of death. Heaven's perfect life is also described in Revelation 22:1–2, where we see "a river of the water of life" and "the tree of life." Heaven is a place of perfect life because we will have perfect, glorified spiritual bodies made like Jesus' glorified body (Philippians 3:21).

According to 1 John 3:2, when we see Christ we will be like Him. This tells us what our bodies are going to be like in heaven. Christ did some remarkable things after He rose from the dead, including traveling anywhere at will despite closed doors or any other obstacle. In our glorified bodies we will have the ability to transport ourselves from one dimension to another simply by deciding to do it.[29]

Part of heaven's perfection and joy will be the chance to say "hello" again to those we have loved, lost, or left behind. I can't wait for that day! In heaven, all the bitterness of saying good-bye will be removed as we delight in relating to one another and to God in ways that we've never experienced on earth.

---

29. Tony Evans, *Tony Evans Speaks Out on Heaven and Hell* (Chicago: Moody Publishers, 2000), 43–44.

FOR FURTHER THOUGHT

What painfulness found here on earth are you most looking forward to not having in heaven?

WILL WE BE BUSY IN HEAVEN?

> No longer will there be any curse. The throne of God and of the Lamb will be in the city, and his servants will serve him.
>
> **—REVELATION 22:3**

I've heard that someone once e-mailed Billy Graham the following note: "To be honest, I'm not even sure I want to go to Heaven. It sounds so boring, just sitting around on a cloud doing nothing." I always admired Dr. Graham for offering clear and practical answers. I'm sure that in this case, he helped the person understand that such views of eternity are based on images from popular culture. Nowhere does the Bible say we will be assigned individual clouds to sit on or harps to play. Instead, passages such as Revelation 22:3 suggest that in heaven we will be given the opportunity to do what we were created to do: serve God.

In heaven our service will not be hindered by distractions, boredom, disinterest, or exhaustion. We can and will serve God forever, and we will find deep satisfaction and purpose in our service.

The unique nature of heaven and its inhabitants will affect the kind of service God requires. Certain types of ministry that are essential in this life—evangelism, to name just one—will be unnecessary in the next. I know that irony was not lost on Billy Graham and his staff. Dr. Graham was fond of telling the story of how his longtime song leader Cliff Barrows would kid him about having a job in heaven while Dr. Graham would be unemployed. With a twinkle in his eye, Barrows would explain that worship leaders will likely be in high demand in heaven. After all, someone has to direct those heavenly choirs! The need for preachers, on the other hand, would seem to be nonexistent.

"I assured him that I wasn't worried about it," Dr. Graham explained, "because I was confident God would find something else for me to do. He might, I added, even change me into a choir director!"

Well-known radio host Hank Hanegraaff has the nickname "The Bible Answer Man." He wrote the following:

> An all-too-prevalent perception in Christianity and the culture is that heaven is going to be one big bore. That, however, is far from true. Rather, heaven will be a place of continuous learning, growth, and development. By nature, humans are finite, and that is how it always will be. While we will have an incredible capacity to learn, we will never come to the end of learning.
>
> To begin with, we will never exhaust exploring our Creator. God by nature is infinite and we are limited. Thus, what we now merely apprehend about the Creator we will spend an eternity seeking to comprehend. Imagine finally beginning to get a handle on how God is one in nature and three in person. Imagine exploring the depths of God's love, wisdom,

and holiness. Imagine forever growing in our capacities to fathom his immensity, immutability, and incomprehensibility. And to top it all off, the more we come to know him, the more there will be to know.

> These are they who have come out of the great tribulation; they have washed their robes and made them white in the blood of the Lamb. Therefore, they are before the throne of God and serve him day and night in his temple; and he who sits on the throne will spread his tent over them. Never again will they hunger; never again will they thirst. The sun will not beat upon them, nor any scorching heat. For the Lamb at the center of the throne will be their shepherd; he will lead them to springs of living water. And God will wipe away every tear from their eyes.
>
> **—REVELATION 7:15–17**

Furthermore, we will never come to the end of exploring fellow Christians. Our ability to appreciate one another will be enhanced exponentially. Imagine being able to love another human being without even a tinge of selfishness. Imagine appreciating, no, reveling in the exalted capacities and station that God bestows on another without so much as a modicum of jealousy.

Finally, we will never come to an end of exploring the Creator's creative handiwork. The universe literally will be our playground. Even if we were capable of exhausting the "new heaven and new earth" (Revelation 21:1), God could create brand new vistas for us to explore.

Will heaven be perfect? Absolutely. Will it be boring? Absolutely not! We will learn without error—but make no mistake about it, *we will learn, we will grow, and we will develop.* Far from being dead and dull, heaven will be an exhilarating, exciting experience that will never come to an end.[30]

I'm encouraged to learn that our activities in heaven will include work and relationships that are enjoyable and fulfilling. We won't race away from the office at the end of the day feeling drained. We will no longer work by the sweat of our brow or fight through weeds and thorns. Instead, our activities will bring us a sense of purpose while we enjoy God and he enjoys us.

FOR FURTHER THOUGHT

If your current job existed in heaven, how might it be made perfect?

WILL HEAVEN BE BORING?

> You make known to me the path of life;
>   you will fill me with joy in your
>   presence,
>   with eternal pleasures at your right
>   hand.

—PSALM 16:11

I remember that as a kid I didn't want to die. It wasn't just that I feared death; it's that I thought heaven would be boring. Heaven,

---

30. Hank Hanegraaff, *The Bible Answer Book* (Nashville: Thomas Nelson, 2004), 141–143.

as it was described to me, sounded like a worship service that would never end. I pictured myself having to stand still—in my best, most uncomfortable clothes—while singing the same boring hymns for eternity. What I didn't understand then (and only glimpse now) is the grand adventure that comes from following God, the true source of fun and adventure. Because life as a Christian on earth is full of joyous adventure, I can only imagine what heaven will be like.

In his book *Things Unseen*, pastor Mark Buchanan described the excitement of heaven:

> Why won't we be bored in heaven? Because it's the one place where both impulses—to go beyond, to go home—are perfectly joined and totally satisfied. It's the one place where we're constantly discovering—where everything is always fresh and the possessing of a thing is as good as the pursuing of it—and yet where we are fully at home—where everything is as it ought to be and where we find, undiminished, that mysterious something we never found down here. . . . And this lifelong melancholy that hangs on us, this wishing we were someone else somewhere else, vanishes too. Our craving to go beyond is always and fully realized. Our yearning for home is once and for all fulfilled. The *ahh!* of deep satisfaction and the *aha!* of delighted surprise meet, and they kiss.[31]

I'm not sure anyone has studied heaven more than Randy Alcorn. He referred to the above quote and added this:

> Our belief that Heaven will be boring betrays a heresy—that God is boring. There's no greater nonsense. Our desire for pleasure and the experience of joy come directly from

---

31. Mark Buchanan, *Things Unseen* (Sisters, OR: Multnomah, 2002). As Quoted in Randy Alcorn, *Heaven* (Wheaton, IL: Tyndale House Publishers, 2004), 394.

> Those who believe that excitement can't exist without sin are thinking with sin-poisoned minds.

WILL HEAVEN BE BORING?

God's hand. He made our taste buds, adrenaline, sex drives, and the nerve endings that convey pleasure to our brains. Likewise, our imaginations and our capacity for joy and exhilaration were made by the very God we accuse of being boring. Are we so arrogant as to imagine that human beings came up with the idea of having fun?

"Won't it be boring to be good all the time?" someone asked. Note the assumption: sin is exciting and righteousness is boring. We've fallen for the devil's lie. His most basic strategy, the same one he employed with Adam and Eve, is to make us believe that sin brings fulfillment. However, in reality, sin robs us of fulfillment. Sin doesn't make life interesting; it makes life empty. Sin doesn't create adventure; it blunts it. Sin doesn't expand life; it shrinks it. Sin's emptiness inevitably leads to boredom. When there's fulfillment, when there's beauty, when we see God as he truly is—an endless reservoir of fascination—boredom becomes impossible.

Those who believe that excitement can't exist without sin are thinking with sin-poisoned minds. Drug addicts are convinced that without their drugs they can't live happy lives. In fact—as everyone else can see—drugs make them miserable. Freedom from sin will mean freedom to be what God intended, freedom to find far greater joy in everything. In Heaven we'll be *filled*—as Psalm 16:11 describes it—with joy and eternal pleasures. . . .

Someone told me nobody will enjoy playing golf in Heaven because it would get boring always hitting holes in one. But why assume everyone's skills will be equal and incapable of further development? Just as our minds will grow in knowledge, our resurrection bodies can develop greater skills.

Another reason people assume Heaven is boring is that their Christian lives are boring. That's not God's fault; it's their own. God calls us to follow him in an adventure that should put us on life's edge. He's infinite in creativity, goodness, beauty, and power. If we're experiencing the invigorating stirrings of God's Spirit, trusting him to fill our lives with divine appointments, experiencing the childlike delights of his gracious daily kindnesses, then we'll know that God is exciting and Heaven is exhilarating. People who love God crave his companionship. To be in his presence will be the very opposite of boredom.

We think of ourselves as fun-loving, and of God as a humorless killjoy. But we've got it backward. It's not God who's boring; it's us. Did we invent wit, humor, and laughter? No. God did. We'll never begin to exhaust God's sense of humor and his love for adventure.[32]

King David wrote, "You make known to me the path of life; you will fill me with joy in your presence, with eternal pleasures at your right hand" (Ps. 16:11). In the presence of God there's nothing but joy. Yes, heaven is a place of praise. But it is also the home of the greatest fun-filled adventure we will ever know.

FOR FURTHER THOUGHT

Where have you found a sense of adventure in your Christian faith?

---

32. Randy Alcorn, *Heaven* (Wheaton, IL: Tyndale House Publishers, 2004), 394–395.

WHAT WILL **SPENDING** **ETERNITY IN HEAVEN** BE LIKE?

> The Son is the radiance of God's glory and the exact representation of his being, sustaining all things by his powerful word. After he had provided purification for sins, he sat down at the right hand of the Majesty in heaven.
>
> **—HEBREWS 1:3**

Have you ever lived a perfectly joyful day? Or received a perfect score on a test? Or held a perfect baby? If you have, then you've experienced brief moments of perfection and happiness. But we all know those moments don't last. Our world and everything in it are perfectly imperfect. So I'm not sure how I'll feel in heaven, in all of its perfection. What will that be like? Consider the words of Jeremy Bouma who is a writer and pastor in Michigan:

> There's an old hymn that says, "When we all get to heaven, what a day of rejoicing that will be! When we all see Jesus, we'll sing and shout the victory!"
>
> This is great news, isn't it? One day we'll finally dwell with God, be with Jesus, shout for joy, and sing of our victory—for all eternity. But what will that experience be like? Have you ever wondered this before?
>
> Many in our culture have tried to answer this question. Pick a scene from a movie or TV show that references the

afterlife and you'll likely find white fluffy clouds, beautiful harp music, lots of singing, streets of gold, shimmering white light, and a Santa-like God with a flowing beard and seated on a throne.

Is this what it will be like to spend eternity in heaven? As appealing as this sounds, the Bible has something surprising to say about what our eternal home will be like.

Surprisingly our hope isn't in heaven per se, although after we die we will go to be with Christ in *heaven* where he dwells. Instead, the Bible makes it clear our hope is in the resurrection on *earth*.

In eternity we won't be floating on clouds, playing harps, singing old hymns, and drinking really bad church coffee—can I get an Amen to that last one? No, our hope is in the resurrection from the dead on a brand new, re-created earth. Perhaps our question should be, What will spending eternity in *heaven-on-earth* be like?

I know this might sound strange, because if you're like me, you grew up hearing that this world is not our home, we're just a passing through. But the end of God's Story says that one day Jesus will return to put our broken, busted world back together again, us included.

What will spending eternity in heaven-on-earth be like, you ask?

First of all, it will be earthly, but in a way that's unimaginably different from now. In Revelation 21 we see God's dwelling place descending to earth, where the first earth will pass away and Christ will make "everything new." Because God will transform this world, no longer will there be death, mourning, crying or pain.

We will also have real bodies again. No, not like zombies, but like Christ! Jesus will transform our bodies so that they will be like his glorious one. And we know from his own

> One day, when we experience heaven's perfection, our perfect moments on earth will feel so small in comparison.

resurrection that our bodies will be like before, but again, unimaginably different.

It will also mean we will spend our time in eternity doing much of the same things we do now. Isaiah 65 gives us a glimpse into this future, saying in heaven-on-earth we will "build houses and dwell in them; [we] will plant vineyards and eat their fruit." This means we'll create things, enjoy our labor, and have really big feasts!

Ultimately, though—and this where the best part comes in—we will spend eternity doing what the heavenly creatures around God's throne are doing right now: serving him and shouting, "Holy, holy, holy is the LORD Almighty; the whole earth is full of his glory" (Isaiah 65:3).

An ancient church creed says, "We look forward to the resurrection of the dead, and to life in the world to come." Amen? Amen![33]

Bouma certainly expresses the hope of heaven. The joys to be found in the life to come are unimaginable and made possible through belief in God's only Son, Jesus. One day when we experience heaven's perfection, our perfect moments on earth will feel so small in comparison.

FOR FURTHER THOUGHT

Can you remember a perfectly blissful moment in your history?

---

33. Adapted from the blog of Jeremy Bouma (www.jeremybouma.com). Used by permission.

Gustave Dore;
The Empyrean, from *The Divine Comedy;*
1857–1868

"There are more things in Heaven and Earth, Horatio, than are dreamt of in your philosophy."

—William Shakespeare, *Hamlet*

"I have come home at last! This is my real country! I belong here. This is the land I have been looking for all my life, though I never knew it till now. . . . Come further up, come further in!"

—C. S. Lewis, *The Last Battle*

"I think Heaven will be like a first kiss."

—Sarah Addison Allen, *The Sugar Queen*

"How sweet is rest after fatigue! How sweet will heaven be when our journey is ended."

—George Whitefield

"I bear my testimony that there is no joy to be found in all this world like that of sweet communion with Christ. I would barter all else there is of heaven for that. Indeed, that is heaven. As for the harps of gold and the streets like clear glass and the songs of seraphs and the shouts of the redeemed, one could very well give all these up, counting them as a drop in a bucket, if we might forever live in fellowship and communion with Jesus."

—Charles H. Spurgeon

"Everything is gone that ever made Jerusalem, like all cities, torn apart, dangerous, heartbreaking, seamy. . . . The city has become what those who loved it always dreamed and what in their dreams she always was. The new Jerusalem. That seems to be the secret of heaven. The new Chicago, Leningrad, Hiroshima, Beirut. The new bus driver, hot-dog man, seamstress, hairdresser. The new you, me, everybody."

—Frederick Buechner

Then I saw "a new heaven and a new earth," for the first heaven and the first earth had passed away, and there was no longer any sea. I saw the Holy City, the new Jerusalem, coming down out of heaven from God, prepared as a bride beautifully dressed for her husband. And I heard a loud voice from the throne saying, "Look! God's dwelling place is now among the people, and he will dwell with them. They will be his people, and God himself will be with them and be their God." . . .

The wall was made of jasper, and the city of pure gold, as pure as glass. The foundations of the city walls were decorated with every kind of precious stone. The first foundation was jasper, the second sapphire, the third agate, the fourth emerald, the fifth onyx, the sixth ruby, the seventh chrysolite, the eighth beryl, the ninth topaz, the tenth turquoise, the eleventh jacinth, and the twelfth amethyst. The twelve gates were twelve pearls, each gate made of a single pearl. The great street of the city was of gold, as pure as transparent glass.

—REVELATION 21:1–3, 18–21

Then the angel showed me the river of the water of life, as clear as crystal, flowing from the throne of God and of the Lamb down the middle of the great street of the city. On each side of the river stood the tree of life, bearing twelve crops of fruit, yielding its fruit every month. And the leaves of the tree are for the healing of the nations. No longer will there be any curse. The throne of God and of the Lamb will be in the city, and his servants will serve him.

—REVELATION 22:1–3

WHERE IS HEAVEN?

And God raised us up with Christ
and seated us with him in the
heavenly realms in Christ Jesus.

—EPHESIANS 2:6

When I think of heaven, like most people, I automatically think of the vast blue sky and the white clouds. If heaven is a place, where exactly is it? Is it in the clouds, past Pluto, in another galaxy? Some people I've talked to think that heaven is simply a state of mind and it's not an actual place. What's the truth?

In *Heaven: Your Real Home*, motivational speaker and courageous survivor Joni Eareckson Tada described it this way:

> I've always sensed that heaven was a lot closer than we are led to believe. As any good child in Sunday school, I believed that heaven was "up." In later years I discovered the Bible says it plainly: Paul was caught *up* to the third heaven . . . Jesus *ascended* into heaven . . . the Lord will catch us *up* into heaven when He returns . . . and, conversely, "God looks *down* from heaven on the sons of men" (Psalm 53:2).
>
> This is the language the Bible invites us to use, much as it encourages us to use other earthbound words like "crowns" or "seas of glass." And it makes sense. Heaven certainly can't be "down" or we'd dig a hole to China.
>
> Yet even though the dwelling place of God may be a long way up, distances like "up" and "down" lose their meaning when you realize that heaven—even the highest heavens—exist beyond our space-time continuum. Latitude and longitude, as well as directions and distances are related to time,

and time is a part of the fourth dimension. And the fourth dimension is only a small part of infinity. Time there will be swallowed up. Step beyond the edge of outer space and you enter the fifth dimension where gargantuan distances light-years long are a snap of the finger to, well . . . to the dying thief who, when he died, instantly appeared in paradise alongside Jesus.

Had I been the dying thief, I would have been dumbstruck to hear Jesus say, "Today, you will be with me in paradise." Today? This instant? Like Jesus taking my hand and walking with me through a wall, as He did in the Upper Room? Or appearing on a beach to cook breakfast for His friends? Or ambling along the road to Emmaus one instant and—flash—arriving in Jerusalem in no time flat? Like being changed in the twinkling of an eye?

Yes, and the Lord gives a clue as to how He does it in Revelation 1:8 when He laughs at time and distance: "'I am the Alpha and Omega,' says the Lord God, 'who is, and who was, and who is to come, the Almighty.'" Notice that Jesus does not follow the convention of our logic about the way time flows; we time-bound creatures want to change the order to read Jesus *was*, is, and is to come. It sounds more chronological. It's consistent with our sense of the past, present, and future. But Jesus is the great "I Am" who always lives in the present. He is the God of the *now*.

I think of this every time I read Revelation 22 when Jesus says three times to the waiting church, "I am coming soon!" (To which the church replies three times, "Come!") It's interesting He doesn't say, "I will come . . . like, sometime around, oh, a couple of thousand years from now." Jesus puts it in the present tense as though He were but a hairsbreadth away, all ready to part the veil of time and distance and step back into our world. It's as though He were on His way back now.

So the kingdom of heaven, over which Jesus *is* and was and ever shall be King, is a place, but more so, a dimension where time and distance are not obstacles. The dying thief wasn't transported at superhuman speed to heaven when he died. Rather, he slipped from one dimension to the next, much like Jesus slipped from one room to another, through walls or whatever. . . .

Even this earth in all its birth pangs is about to give one last grunt and find itself born as a "new earth" in heaven. Actually, this moment, less than a hairsbreadth separates this material world from the spiritual world that is embracing earth. And like an unborn baby, we are being fashioned for the greater world into which we are about to be born (by dying, of all things!). We have a hard time believing that heaven encompasses this world, and so the Bible has to keep prodding us to fix our eyes "not on what is seen, but what is unseen." It's a matter of "seeing." Using our eyes of faith.

Faith assures us that heaven is *transcendent*. It is beyond the limits of our experience; it exists apart from our material universe. Heaven is also *immanent* in that it envelopes all the celestial bodies, swirling galaxies, and the starry hosts. If we believe that God is omnipresent, then we can at least believe that what the Bible in Ephesians 2:6 calls the heavenly realms are omnipresent, as well. For where God is, the kingdom of heaven is.[34]

Heaven is more than a state of mind; it's an actual place. Joni Eareckson Tada calls it "your real home." It's the place where God dwells, and so it's the place where we will finally find the peace that we seek here on earth.

---

34. Joni Eareckson Tada, *Heaven: Your Real Home* (Grand Rapids: Zondervan, 2010), 78–80.

FOR FURTHER THOUGHT

If heaven, not this world, is your real home, how could that motivate your actions today?

IS HEAVEN A REAL PLACE?

> May you be blessed by the LORD,
> the Maker of heaven and earth.
>
> **—PSALM 115:15**

When friends return from amazing vacations, they will tell stories and share pictures about the places they visited. But somehow, no matter how many stories I hear or pictures I see, these amazing earthly places just don't feel real until I actually see them with my own eyes. I will need to climb the ancient steps of Machu Picchu and listen to a bird-filled jungle before I will truly understand how beautiful those places are. In the same way, while I enjoy hearing stories and tales that offer glimpses of heaven, I know that we will not fully understand how beautiful it is until we see it ourselves.

Here's what Wayne Grudem, one of the most well-known Christian teachers of our time, has said about heaven:

> After the final judgment, believers will enter into the full enjoyment of life in the presence of God forever. Jesus will say to us, "Come, O blessed of my Father, inherit the kingdom prepared for you from the foundation of the world"

What the Bible Says About Heaven

A Rainbow Encircles the Throne
Ezekiel 1:26–28; Revelation 4:3

God's Heavenly Throne
Psalm 11:4

Myriad of Angels
Revelation 5:11–13

Sea of Glass Glowing with Fire
Revelation 15:2–3

Golden Altar in Front of the Throne
Revelation 8:3

Heavenly Door
Revelation 4:1

Tribulation Elders in White Robes
Revelation 7:13–17

Twenty-Four Elders on Twenty-Four Thrones Dressed in White with Crowns of Gold on Their Heads
Revelation 4:4

Winged Living Creatures Covered in Eyes
Revelation 4:6–11

The Souls of the Martyrs Under the Altar
Revelation 6:9

Seraphim Worshiping God
Isaiah 6:1–3

Seven Sealed Scrolls
Revelation 5:1–5

Seven Spirits Before the Throne
Revelation 1:4

© TheBiblePeople.com

(Matt. 25:34). We will enter a kingdom where "there shall no more be anything accursed, but the throne of God and of the Lamb shall be in it, and his servants shall worship him" (Rev. 22:3).

When referring to this place, Christians often talk about living with God "in heaven" forever. But in fact the biblical teaching is richer than that: it tells us that there will be new heavens *and a new earth*—an entirely renewed creation— and we will live with God there.

The Lord promises through Isaiah, "For behold, I create new heavens and a new earth; and the former things shall not be remembered" (Isa. 65:17), and speaks of "the new heavens and the new earth which I will make" (Isa. 66:22). . . . In John's vision of events to follow the final judgment, he says, "Then I saw a new heaven and a new earth; heaven and the first earth had passed away" (Rev. 21:1). He goes on to tell us that there will also be a new kind of unification of heaven and earth, for he sees the holy city, the "new Jerusalem," coming "down out of heaven from God" (Rev. 21:2), and hears a voice proclaiming that "the dwelling of God is with men. He will dwell with them, and they shall be his people, and God himself will be with them" (v. 3). So there will be a joining of heaven and earth in this new creation, and there we will live in the presence of God.

During this present age, the place where God dwells is frequently called "heaven" in Scripture. The Lord says, "Heaven is my throne" (Isa. 66:1), and Jesus teaches us to pray, "Our Father who art in heaven" (Matt. 6:9). Jesus now "has gone into heaven, and is at the right hand of God" (1 Peter 3:22). In fact, heaven may be defined as follows: *Heaven is the place where God most fully makes known His presence to bless* . . . where he makes his glory known, and where angels, other heavenly creatures, and redeemed saints all worship him.

But someone may wonder how heaven can be joined together with earth. Clearly the earth is a place that exists at a certain location in our space-time universe, but can heaven also be thought of as a place that can be joined to the earth?

The New Testament teaches the idea of a location for heaven in several different ways, and quite clearly. When Jesus ascended into heaven, the fact that he went to a place seems to be the entire point of the narrative, and the point that Jesus intended his disciples to understand by the way in which he gradually ascended even while speaking to them: "As they were looking on, he was lifted up, and a cloud took him out of their sight" (Acts 1:9; cf. Luke 24:51: "While he blessed them, he parted from them"). The angels exclaimed, "This Jesus, who was taken up from you into heaven, will come in the same way as you saw him go into heaven" (Acts 1:11). It is hard to imagine how the fact of Jesus' ascension to a place could be taught more clearly.[35]

Heaven is real, and it is a place beyond my wildest imagination. It's better than anything I have experienced here on earth: better than my children being born, better than the reddest sunset or the fullest moon. I can't imagine a better place.

FOR FURTHER THOUGHT

Do cynicism and bitterness keep you from believing that heaven is real?

---

35. Wayne Grudem, *Heaven and Hell, A Zondervan Digital Short* (Grand Rapids: Zondervan, 2012).

IS HEAVEN **ETERNAL?**

If someone dies, will they live again?
All the days of my hard service
I will wait for my renewal to come.

—JOB 14:14

I fell in love with my wife during our college years, and ever since then I've never been able to imagine life without her. Since our first day together, I've wanted to be with her forever. As 1980s pop icon Sheena Easton has sung: "Darling, you be the only one for me, together for eternity."[36] Isn't the idea of "forever" comforting? We crave lasting security. We want to know that whatever goes wrong, we will always have each other.

And while my wife and I may commit to each other for a lifetime, eventually one of us—and then eventually both of us—will die. Though we have good intentions, we really don't have a good grasp on eternity or an eternal commitment. So, what about heaven? Can we really rely on that? Will it truly last for eternity?

James D. Kennedy, an American pastor and Christian broadcaster, wrote this before he died:

> More than thirteen hundred years ago in the portion of England known as Northumbria, the first Christian missionaries arrived. They came to the courts of King Edwin of Northumbria, and in his great hall ablaze with the light

---

36. http://www.songlyrics.com/sheena-easton/eternity-lyrics/.

of many torches, huge logs in the fireplace, and grizzled chieftains surrounding them, these Christian missionaries gave their first discourse on the Christian faith. When they had finished, one asked, "Can this new religion tell us anything of what happens after death? The soul of man is like a sparrow flying through this lighted hall. It enters at one door from the darkness outside, flits through the light and warmth, and passes out at the further end into the dark again. Can this new religion solve for us the mystery?"[37]

I, for one, am convinced that this new religion, now old with age, is the only one that can give us any sure and certain word concerning life after death. I believe in immortality; I believe in heaven. The reasons are manifold. Not all of them have the same weight in my mind or the minds of any other individuals, of course, but together they form the threads of what I believe is an exceedingly strong cord.

First of all, let us consider an argument from the realm of science. The first law of thermodynamics states that energy or matter cannot be created or destroyed. They may be transformed one into the other, but they cannot be destroyed. This was set forth by Einstein and was conclusively demonstrated at Hiroshima. Burris Jenkins put it this way: "No single atom in creation can go out of existence, according to the scientists; it only changes in form. We cannot burn up anything; we simply change it from a solid to a gaseous state. Neither is any energy or force ever destroyed; it is only changed from one form to another."[38] If man ceases to exist, he will be the only thing in this universe that does.

---

37. Leslie D. Weatherhead, *After Death* (New York: Abingdon Press, 1936), 19.

38. Thomas Curtis Clark, ed., *The Golden Book of Immortality* (New York: Association Press, 1954), 4.

Therefore, to begin with, there is the probability that we shall continue to exist.

Second, let us consider this analogy from nature. It has probably never been stated any better than by William Jennings Bryan in his *Analogies of Nature*:

> Christ gave us proof of immortality, and yet it would hardly seem necessary that one should rise from the dead to convince us that the grave is not the end. If the Father deigns to touch with Divine power the cold and pulseless heart of the buried acorn and to make it burst forth into a new life, will He leave neglected in the earth the soul of man, made in the image of his Creator? . . . No, I am as sure that there is another life as I am that I live today![39]

Third, there is the universal longing of mankind for eternity. . . .

What is the explanation? I believe the Scriptures give to us very clearly the fact that God has placed immortality—eternity—in the breast of man. He only of all of God's creation longs for eternal life. This longing is found everywhere. It is a universal experience of mankind that forbids him to accept any other answer to the riddle of life. Emerson said, "The blazing evidence of immortality is our dissatisfaction with any other solution."[40, 41]

Think about it. If God is in love with the people he created to love, why would he want to ever be apart from us? God is constantly communicating his love to us more powerfully than

---

39. Madison C. Peters, *After Death—What?* (New York: Christian Herald, 1908), 165.

40. Quoted in Weatherhead, *After Death*, 22.

41. James Kennedy, *Why I Believe* (Nashville: Thomas Nelson, 2005), 74–76.

any pop song or romantic poem ever could. One day, he will personally show us what eternal love really means.

FOR FURTHER THOUGHT

Does the idea of spending an eternity in heaven scare or comfort you?

 ## WHAT IS THE "NEW HEAVEN"?

> Then I saw "a new heaven and a new earth," for the first heaven and the first earth had passed away, and there was no longer any sea.
>
> **—REVELATION 21:1**

Do you know the expression "If it seems too good to be true, it probably is"? I know this expression well. Like most of us, I've experienced my share of troubles and pain. Many of us believe that nothing will ever get any better here on earth and that this life is all there is. But is that the truth? What if there was a new heaven and a new earth with a new you and a new me waiting to live in them?

John MacArthur, preacher and teacher, wrote the following:

We return to Revelation 21 for a biblical description of the "new heaven and a new earth: for the first heaven and the first earth were passed away" (v. 1). The Greek word translated "new" (*kainos*) stresses that the earth God will create will not just be "new" as opposed to "old." It will also be *different*. Paul uses the same Greek word in 2 Corinthians 5:17: "If any man be in Christ, he is a new creature." It speaks of a change in quality. The new heavens and earth, like our newness in Christ, will be glorified, free from sin's curse, and eternal.

Scripture doesn't tell us what the new earth will look like, but we have reason to believe that it will in many respects be familiar. Jerusalem will be there—albeit an all-new Jerusalem. John's description concentrates on the Holy City, which has streets, and walls, and gates. John also mentions a high mountain, water, a stream, and trees. Best of all it is populated with the people of God—real people we will know and with whom we will share eternal fellowship.

The new earth will also be utterly different, unfamiliar. John says, for example, "there will be no more sea" (Rev. 21:1). That's a significant difference immediately, because the current earth is covered mostly with water. Some Bible scholars think this stresses the erasure of all national boundaries. Others point out that the sea symbolized fear to the ancients, so they believe the absence of sea implies the absence of fear. Both may be true. In the new heaven and earth nothing will make us afraid, and nothing will separate us from other people. The only water described in heaven is "a pure river of water of life, clear as crystal, proceeding out of the throne of God and of the Lamb" (Rev. 22:1). This crystal-clear river flows right down heaven's main street (v. 2).

Revelation 21:3–7 outlines the most remarkable features of the New Heavens and New Earth:

> *And I heard a great voice out of heaven saying, Behold, the tabernacle of God is with men, and he will dwell with them, and they shall be his people, and*

*God himself shall be with them, and be their God.
And God shall wipe away all tears from their eyes;
and there shall be no more death, neither sorrow, nor
crying, neither shall there be any more pain: for the
former things are passed away. And he that sat upon
the throne said, Behold, I make all things new. And
he said unto me, Write: for these words are true and
faithful. And he said unto me, It is done. I am Alpha
and Omega, the beginning and the end. I will give
unto him that is athirst of the fountain of the water of
life freely. He that overcometh shall inherit all things;
and I will be his God, and he shall be my son.*

Here Scripture promises that heaven will be a realm of perfect bliss. Tears, pain, sorrow, and crying will have no place whatsoever in the New Heaven and New Earth. It is a place where God's people will dwell together with Him eternally, utterly free from all the effects of sin and evil. God is pictured as personally wiping away the tears from the eyes of the redeemed.

Heaven is a realm where death is fully conquered (1 Cor. 15:26). There is no sickness there, no hunger, no trouble, and no tragedy. Just absolute joy and eternal blessings. It is frankly hard for our minds, which have never known anything but this sinful life and its calamities, to imagine.[42]

I know this much is true: God has greater ideas in his mind than I have in mine. I can't always imagine a better earth, but God can, and he has plans to bring it into reality. He has in his heart and mind the vision of a new heaven and a new earth.

---

42. Taken from *The Glory of Heaven* by John MacArthur, © 1996, pp. 95–96. Used by permission of Crossway, a publishing ministry of Good News Publishers, Wheaton, IL 60187, www.crossway.org.

This will be a place without any sadness or heartache, where tragedy will be swept away. I can't wait for that day, can you?

FOR FURTHER THOUGHT

Why do you think God wants to restore the "old" heaven and earth instead of making something completely new?

WHAT WILL HEAVEN'S NEW JERUSALEM BE LIKE?

> Also in front of the throne there was what looked like a sea of glass, clear as crystal. In the center, around the throne, were four living creatures, and they were covered with eyes, in front and in back.
>
> **—REVELATION 4:6**

What's your favorite place on earth? I love Washington Island in Door County, Wisconsin. The clear and brightly sparkling water reminds me of references to heaven's crystal sea that sits in front of the throne of God in heaven. It's hard for me not to think about heaven as I watch the sun sparkle off the water surrounding Washington Island. The Bible describes heaven as a place that will also be home to the new, beautiful city of Jerusalem.

Randy Alcorn described his view of the New Jerusalem in heaven this way:

The New Jerusalem will be a place of extravagant beauty and natural wonders. It will be a vast Eden, integrated with the best of human culture, under the reign of Christ. More wealth than has been accumulated in all human history will be spread freely across this immense city.

Presumably many other cities will be on the New Earth, such as those Jesus mentioned in the stewardship parables (Luke 19:17–19). The kings of nations who bring their treasures into the New Jerusalem must come from and return to somewhere, presumably countryside and cities lying beyond the New Jerusalem. But no city will be like this one, for it will be called home by the King of kings.

Heaven's capital city will be filled with visual magnificence. "It shone with the glory of God, and its brilliance was like that of a very precious jewel, like a jasper, clear as crystal" (Revelation 21:11). John goes on to describe the opulence: "The wall was made of jasper, and the city of pure gold, as pure as glass. The foundations of the city walls were decorated with every kind of precious stone" (Revelation 21:18–19). John then names twelve stones, eight of which correspond to the stones of the high priest's breastpiece (Exodus 28:17–20).

The precious stones and gold represent incredible wealth, suggestive of the exorbitant riches of God's splendor. "The twelve gates were twelve pearls, each gate made of a single pearl. The great street of the city was of pure gold, like transparent glass" (Revelation 21:21). Each gate tower is carved from a single, huge pearl. "Among the ancients, the pearl was highest in value among the precious stones."[43] The text doesn't say this, but commentators often suggest that because a pearl is formed through the oyster's pain, the pearl

43. Steven J. Lawson, *Heaven Help Us!* (Colorado Springs: NavPress, 1995), 131.

may symbolize Christ's suffering on our behalf as well as the eternal beauty that can come out of our temporary suffering.

John describes a natural wonder in the center of the New Jerusalem: "the river of the water of life, as clear as crystal, flowing from the throne of God and of the Lamb down the middle of the great street of the city" (Revelation 22:1–2). Why is water important? Because the city is a center of human life and water is an essential part of life. Ghosts don't need water, but human bodies do. We all know what it's like to be thirsty, but the original readers, who lived in a bone-dry climate, readily grasped the wonder of constantly available fresh water, pure and uncontaminated, able to satisfy the deepest thirst.

Notice that the source of this powerful stream is the throne of God, occupied by the Lamb. He's the source of all natural beauties and wonders. They derive their beauty from the Artist. The great river reflects his thirst-quenching, need-satisfying nature. He always meets his people's needs and fulfills their longings.

On the New Earth, we won't have to leave the city to find natural beauty. It will be incorporated into the city, with the river of life as its source. The river flows down the city's main street. Likely it has countless tributaries flowing throughout the rest of the city. Can you picture people talking and laughing beside this river, sticking their hands and faces down into the water and drinking? This fully accessible natural wonder on the city's main street is amazing—something that would be featured in any travel brochure.[44]

Streets of gold, gates of pearls, and walls of gems sound better than blacktop and asphalt, don't they? Every city on earth will be made new when God's rule and reign comes to earth.

---

44. Randy Alcorn, *Heaven* (Wheaton, IL: Tyndale House Publishers, 2004), 247–248.

The New Jerusalem

Revelation 21:10—22:2

12 gates with names of 12 tribes of Israel

12 foundations with names of 12 apostles

City is shaped like a cube

12 angels at the gates

Walls of jasper; city of gold

Foundations of walls decorated with 12 kinds of jewels

Pearl gates; gold street

Temple is God and the Lamb

No moon or sun because the glory of God and the Lamb provide light

Only those whose names are written in the Lamb's book of life can enter

River of life flows from the throne of God and the Lamb

Tree of life stands on each side of the river

The New Jerusalem won't be like the earthly Jerusalem that we hear about on the news. There won't be bombings inside of it, dust on its streets, or hatred among people. Now that's something to live for.

FOR FURTHER THOUGHT

How do you envision a perfect city in heaven?

WILL WE REMEMBER THE PAIN AND SUFFERING WE EXPERIENCED ON EARTH?

> I have told you these things, so that in me you may have peace. In this world you will have trouble. But take heart! I have overcome the world.
>
> **—JOHN 16:33**

The twentieth century was the century of refugees, conflicts, and disasters—literal hells on earth. From the Holocaust in Europe to the killing fields of Cambodia to the atomic bombs dropped in Japan, there has been no shortage of human suffering. One thing that I have wondered about heaven is whether we will remember the pain and suffering that we experienced on earth.

Author and pastor David Swanson shared his perspective on this in *What Is Heaven Like?*:

When we move into our immortal state and take up residence in the heavenly realms, all suffering will end. I think this may well be what people look forward to the most, because we all know what it is to suffer, and to suffer acutely. God promises us that we will have trouble in this world, but he also says he has overcome the world (John 16:33). He tells us that if the world hated him, it will also hate us (John 15:18). This world is a hard place to live in, but heaven is the opposite of that. Revelation 21:4 reminds us, "He will wipe every tear from their eyes. There will be no more death or mourning or crying or pain, for the old order of things has passed away." The old way of the world—living with suffering and evil—is gone.

In heaven mourning and grief are nonexistent because death does not exist. All tears are wiped from our eyes because there is nothing and no one left to wound us. We are no longer separated from our loved ones. There is no more crying, no more pain, no more physical illness or limitation. Cancer is done—over. Chemotherapy never again has to be endured. There is no more heart disease or heart attacks. No more autism or Down syndrome. No more diabetes or Crohn's disease or diverticulitis. No more depression or anxiety or schizophrenia or bipolar disorder. No more hunger, thirst, or famine. There is no more poverty.

In the glory of heaven, it's all over and done with because Christ took all that suffering and pain on himself at the cross. I think it's an important point for us to consider here . . . 85 percent of Americans believe in heaven, but relatively few consider the question about whether they will go there when they die. I find that so odd. Scripture makes it plain that you don't go to heaven unless you are in Christ, redeemed by his blood. It is a thought often left out in our greeting-card world. Songwriter Julie Gold writes in a song about heaven, "I think I'll go to heaven, there I will lay me down."[45] I love the song, but the sentiment is wrong. You can't just say, "I think I'll go." It's more than that. You go only if you are accompanied by the one who opened the way. George Matheson put it this way in his hymn "O Love That Will Not Let Me Go": O Cross that liftest up my head, I dare not ask to fly from thee; I lay in dust life's glory dead, and from the ground there blossoms red life that shall endless be.[46] The ground of heaven blossoms red from the blood-stained ground of the cross, granting us an eternal inheritance far beyond what we can ever imagine. Our suffering is gone because his suffering has been offered on our behalf. It is only by his blood that we ever enter therein, which is why God's call on our life to share the Good News is so vitally important. The lives of many hang in the balance today, and they will never know the glorious hope of heaven unless we share Jesus with them. . . .

Jewish psychiatrist Victor Frankl, arrested and imprisoned by the Nazis in World War II, wrote a book called *Man's Search for Meaning*, in which he discussed the manner in which human beings deal with suffering. He described, sometimes in disturbing detail, the way his fellow prisoners coped with the hardship of their lives. Some gave up, yet others managed to survive even though they were stripped of every shred of human dignity. He wrote, "There is nothing in the world . . . that would so effectively help one to survive even the worst conditions as the knowledge that there is a meaning in one's life."[47] . . . In the words of Nietzsche: He who has a *why* to live for can bear almost any *how*. The *why*

---

45. Julie Gold, "Heaven," from *Dream Loud*, Gadfly Records, 1998.

46. George Matheson, "O Love That Wilt Not Let Me Go," Church of Scotland, January 1882.

47. Victor Frankl, *Man's Search for Meaning* (New York: Pocket Books, 1997), 25.

for Christians is the fulfilling of the plan of God's ultimate kingdom and the knowledge that one day we will inhabit that place in all its eternal fullness. Frankl's point is that our ability to endure suffering is far greater when we have hope.[48]

Heaven is the opposite of the hells on earth that many people have experienced. We know from the Bible that heaven will not contain any sorrow or pain. And although we do not have the answer about what we will remember, we can rest assured that memories that were once painful will no longer be so. God promises to remove every tear from our tear ducts and every trauma from our minds.

FOR FURTHER THOUGHT

Do you think you will still be fully who you are in heaven if you do not remember certain experiences that you had while on earth?

WHY CAN'T WE UNDERSTAND HEAVEN?

"What no eye has seen,
    what no ear has heard,
and what no human mind has
    conceived"—

---

48. David D. Swanson, *What Is Heaven Like?*, Baker Books, a division of Baker Publishing Group, 2013, 158. Used by permission.

> the things God has prepared for
> those who love him.
>
> **—1 CORINTHIANS 2:9**

When my son was about twelve months old, he would toddle around and say "dis" for "this." He would point at objects in this new and unfamiliar world, asking me to give him the words to describe them. "Ball," I would say, or "dog" or "flower." Eventually, like all children, he gained the language he needed to talk about the world around him.

Imagine not having the language to describe the world. A sense of frustration and even fear results for children who do not acquire language at a normal rate of development. Is it possible that we cannot understand heaven because, like small children, we have not yet been given the language and the necessary knowledge?

Author and Moody Bible Institute professor John Koessler explained it this way:

> My anxiety about heaven diminished as I continued to read the Bible. I began to understand that the images the Scriptures used of heaven were intentionally earthly, employing the language of the ordinary to describe the eternal. The angelic beings that surround the throne of God combine elements that are common to earthly creatures, making them terrifying in their familiarity (Rev. 4:7; cf. Ezek. 1:10). The architecture of heaven, according to Scripture, is rife with beautiful gems and precious metals (Rev. 21:18–21).
>
> C. S. Lewis explains the necessity for this language: "Heaven is, by definition, outside our experience, but all intelligible descriptions must be of things within our experience."

Earthly experience is the only experience we know and must be our starting point when speaking of heaven.

The earthly images that God has embedded in human experience and Scripture speak to us of heaven but cannot take us there. They carry the fragrance of heaven with them but that is all. Still, these biblical images, coupled with our own earthly experiences, can help us anticipate what is to come. The Bible draws on our experience to paint a picture that mirrors the true reality of heaven, but only in broad strokes. We do not see its towers and spires with clarity. Rather, we see "through a glass darkly," a poor reflection in a dim mirror (1 Cor. 13:12). Those who seek heaven in the images eventually find only dust and ashes.

The fault may lie with human language. Perhaps it is too narrow a palette to hold all the colors of heaven. We who have not experienced heaven cannot know what it is truly like. If it is true that language must use human experience as its point of reference, then the images of the Bible and our experience can move only in one direction, arguing from the lesser to the greater.

But ultimately the problem lies elsewhere. Jesus' criticism of Nicodemus in John 3:12 is equally true of us: "I have spoken to you of earthly things and you do not believe; how then will you believe if I speak of heavenly things?" There is a high likelihood that we would not believe, even if the language could be found to tell us. . . .

This is the dilemma we face when it comes to being heavenly minded. It is hard to think of heaven without thinking of earth. Our earthly reality seems so much more tangible; we barely know what awaits us in heaven, and can't really know what we are missing. "No eye has seen," the apostle Paul assures us, "no ear has heard, no mind has conceived what God has prepared for those who love him" (1 Cor. 2:9).

It is hard to wait for what we cannot see; harder yet to long for what we do not know. Fortunately for us, the apostle goes on to say that God has revealed these things to us by his Spirit. Like a bride so eager for her wedding night that the faded picture of her lover will kindle the fire of desire, we too are surrounded by images designed to ignite our longing for heaven. They are only shadows and not the reality of the life that is to come. But for now, they are enough.[49]

Like small children who see a flower but do not yet know the name for it, nor understand its components or recognize its fragrance, we cannot fully understand heaven because it is outside our experience. I don't know about you, but I know for myself that the few glimpses I've had of heaven here on earth make me excited to see what God has prepared for us in the world to come!

FOR FURTHER THOUGHT

What are some glimpses that you've had of heaven here on earth?

---

49. John Koessler, "Come, Lord Jesus—But Not Too Soon," *Christianity Today* (September 2005).

RESIDENTS OF HEAVEN

Hans Memling; *The Last Judgment* (detail); 1467–1471

"I don't like to commit myself about heaven and hell—you see, I have friends in both places."

    —Mark Twain

"I don't want to go to heaven. None of my friends are there."

    —Oscar Wilde

"Good girls go to heaven, bad girls go everywhere."

    —Katharine Hepburn, *Me: Stories of My Life*

"If there are no dogs in Heaven, then when I die I want to go where they went."

    —Will Rogers

"He didn't want you to be alone . . . He would rather go to hell for you than to heaven without you."

    —Max Lucado

"We may be surprised at the people we find in heaven. God has a soft spot for sinners. His standards are quite low."

    —Desmond Tutu

"God will prepare everything for our perfect happiness in heaven, and if it takes my dog being there, I believe he'll be there."

—Billy Graham

He who was seated on the throne said, "I am making everything new!" Then he said, "Write this down, for these words are trustworthy and true."

He said to me: "It is done. I am the Alpha and the Omega, the Beginning and the End. To the thirsty I will give water without cost from the spring of the water of life. Those who are victorious will inherit all this, and I will be their God and they will be my children. But the cowardly, the unbelieving, the vile, the murderers, the sexually immoral, those who practice magic arts, the idolaters and all liars—they will be consigned to the fiery lake of burning sulfur. This is the second death."

—REVELATION 21:5–8

WILL I BE WITH THE PEOPLE I KNOW IN HEAVEN?

> And just as we have borne the image of the earthly man, so shall we bear the image of the heavenly man.
>
> **—1 CORINTHIANS 15:49**

Have you ever been to a family reunion? Going to my wife's family reunion for the first time was an eye opener. I met people I had only heard about. I put faces and names with some of the legendary stories my wife had shared with me. It was a time to discover things about my wife, her history, and even more about our new life together. Have you ever considered that heaven will be like a family reunion, full of joy and discovery yet void of the awkward and strained relationships that you had on earth?

Dr. Dan Lockwood is an author and former president of Multnomah University. When reflecting on heaven, he said the following:

> Does the Bible teach that we will recognize our loved ones in heaven? As the years pass, this question looms larger in my thinking. Last year, I attended three funeral services of godly saints who'd passed away. One was my 85-year-old father-in-law, whose exemplary life and witness is now just a cherished memory. For my wife, who loved her father dearly, this question is thus no idle theological speculation. Fortunately, the Bible speaks clearly to it.

The simple answer—yes—rests on two pillars of Christian belief. One is the blessed hope that we will see Jesus again (Titus 2:13). The other is the assurance that our present bodies will be raised from the dead, immortal (1 Cor. 15:12-57). Together, these pillars provide a basis for believing we will recognize our loved ones in heaven. After all, if we can recognize the Lord Jesus, possessing the perfectly restored and glorified bodies to do so, it follows that we will recognize other believers, including our loved ones.

But to give more biblical shape and substance to this answer, we must distinguish between our temporary dwelling in heaven (our "intermediate state") and our eternal home in the new heaven and new earth (our ultimate destiny). Consider the following two propositions.

First, when we die, we are consciously and immediately in the presence of our Savior in heaven.

The Bible is clear that after death, two literal destinies await all humanity: eternal life and eternal death (Rom. 6:23). Those who place their faith in Jesus Christ receive everlasting life. When a believer dies, her body remains in the grave, but her soul is consciously and immediately taken into the presence of Jesus. Our soul's immediate destiny is heaven, since Jesus himself ascended into heaven (Acts 1:11) and is presently there preparing dwelling places for us (John 14:1-3).

One passage that makes it clear we are conscious with Jesus after we die is Revelation 6:9-11. There the souls of tribulation martyrs in heaven ask the Lord how long it will be until their righteous blood is avenged. Apparently without resurrected bodies yet, they are still fully conscious, having speech and recollection.

That we are immediately with Jesus after death is implicit in at least two passages: Jesus' words to the dying thief, "Today you will be with me in paradise" (Luke 23:43), and Paul's conviction that "we would prefer to be away from the body and at home with the Lord" (2 Cor. 5:8). Neither Jesus nor the apostle foresaw centuries of separation while our bodies lay in graves, awaiting the final resurrection. Rather, they anticipated an immediate reunion!

We can anticipate that as well. Though without our physical bodies, we will be able to commune with Jesus, with Abraham, and with believing loved ones who have preceded us to heaven.

Second, when Jesus returns, we will receive our resurrected bodies and live with him forever in the new heaven and new earth.

The cornerstone of all eschatological hope is the Second Coming of Jesus Christ. At that moment, not before, believers in Jesus will receive their resurrected, immortal bodies: The dead in Christ will be raised and living saints will be caught up ("raptured") to meet Christ (1 Thess. 4:15-17). All who see Christ face to face shall, in that moment, become like him (1 John 3:2).

Our resurrection bodies are not merely immortal duplicates of our present ones. Consider Paul's analogy of the wheat seed (1 Cor. 15:35-38). A mortal body is like the seed, while an immortal body is like the full-grown plant. Both are physical, with an intrinsic continuity between the two. But what a difference between the seed and the plant in appearance, in attribute, and in potential! If we presently have the capacity to recognize our loved ones, that ability will be magnified, not lessened, in the immortal state.

It is in these extraordinary bodies that we will dwell together with Christ for all eternity in the new earth (Rev. 21:1-22:6). There, we will commune not only with the exalted

> A mortal body is like the seed,
> while an immortal body is
> like the full-grown plant.

Christ, but also with all those who are numbered among his children, including our believing loved ones.

Of course, there are many unanswerable questions about our glorified bodies and the life to come. How old will we appear? Will we all be equally strong or smart? How can we possibly be happy without marriage?

But the answer to whether we'll recognize our departed loved ones now residing in heaven is as certain as our assurance of seeing our Savior.[50]

I am excited to experience heaven's great reunion. I take great comfort in knowing that I will one day see the people I've loved and lost. We'll be together this time, never to be separated again.

FOR FURTHER THOUGHT

Whom are you looking forward to seeing in heaven?

50. Lockwood, Daniel. "Until We Meet Again." *Christianity Today* (October 2007). Used by permission of the author.

DO **UNBORN** CHILDREN OR THOSE WHO DIE **YOUNG** GO TO **HEAVEN**?

> Then people brought little children to Jesus for him to place his hands on them and pray for them. But the disciples rebuked them. Jesus said, "Let the little children come to me, and do not hinder them, for the kingdom of heaven belongs to such as these."
>
> **—MATTHEW 19:13–14**

When I ask what people wonder about heaven, one of the most frequent questions I hear is this: "What about children who were aborted, or children who had special mental challenges which hindered their ability to make a choice? Will they go to heaven?" Oftentimes, behind this question is a father or mother who has experienced heartbreak, and sometimes regret. It's a question that our hearts want to answer with, "Of course!" But what do the facts say? What does the Bible say? And what about the deeper question behind it: At what point and under what circumstances does God hold people accountable for their choices?

In his book *Safe in the Arms of God*, popular Bible teacher John MacArthur has provided his views on the age of accountability:

In certain church circles, the question is often couched in this way: "What is the age of accountability?"

The issue is not truly one of "age" but rather "condition." I have baptized young people who have told me that they believe they were saved at the age of ten, or twelve, or eight. There is no one age at which every person suddenly becomes accountable for knowing the difference between sin and righteousness, judgment and forgiveness, and understanding the gospel. All children are unique in their development and exposure to the truth. There is no one age in the Bible at which all children are declared to be "accountable." Neither is there one chronological age in a person's life in which a person suddenly and automatically knows right from wrong or is capable of understanding God's plan for salvation.

The condition of accountability is what matters. Every infant or child who dies before reaching a condition of moral culpability goes instantly to heaven at death. . . .

Only God knows the time when a child becomes "accountable." The reason Scripture includes one account of Jesus between His infancy and adulthood, at the age of twelve, is to show that He had come to a full understanding of His divine nature and His personal mission. When He told His earthly parents, who had been looking for Him, "I must be about My Father's business," He was informing them, at the age of twelve, of His full awareness of the realities of His life as the Son of God. And that is a good general age to look for the condition of accountability. . . .

A miscarried or aborted baby has no understanding of law and grace, sin and salvation. Neither does a baby who dies at birth or shortly thereafter. Neither does an infant. Neither does a toddler or young child—or even an older child, in some cases.

At some point in a child's maturation, he or she comes to have an understanding of law and grace. In other words, the child begins to comprehend and *understand* these principles:

God has rules and commandments; sin involves the violation or breaking of God's laws; forgiveness of sin has been made possible through the death of Jesus Christ on the cross; the grace of God allows for all who believe in and receive Jesus Christ as their Savior and submit to Him as Lord to be cleansed of their sin and live in the newness of life and joyful obedience to Him.

From child to child, that precise age varies. It is the "condition" that counts, not a calendar.

Some children, of course, never reach such a level of maturation. They are mentally impaired to the point that they are forever locked into thinking as a young child thinks—we might say they "have the mind of a five-year-old" or they are "like a child" in their mental capacities related to reasoning, remembering, or making moral choices. Their bodies may mature fully, but their minds do not. These, too, are "children" who may never reach a condition of moral culpability.[51]

Eric Clapton's famous song after the death of his four-year-old son asks, "Would you know my name if I saw you in heaven?"[52]

I am comforted to know that heaven is a place where we will find children safe in the arms of God, the one who made them and enjoys spending time with them.

---

51. John MacArthur, *Safe in the Arms of God* (Nashville: Thomas Nelson, 2003), 36–38.

52. http://www.metrolyrics.com/tears-in-heaven-lyrics-eric-clapton.html.

FOR FURTHER THOUGHT

What children do you know who may be coming to the age of moral accountability?

WILL THERE BE ANIMALS IN HEAVEN?

> I saw heaven standing open and there before me was a white horse, whose rider is called Faithful and True. With justice he judges and wages war.
>
> **—REVELATION 19:11**

When I was a little boy, I had a beloved hamster named Squeaky. This remarkably smart animal would escape his cage most nights, retrieve a toy from my shelves, and carry it back to his cage. Most mornings, I would awake to find a baseball card, an action figure, or another gadget in his cage. One morning I discovered that he had made a soft-looking bed out of a miniature American flag I had kept on my desk. Like most children, I was devastated when my favorite pet died! I cried and cried. My parents told me that I would see him in heaven, but is that true? I've heard people say that there won't be any animals in the next life, but doesn't the Bible say that Jesus will return on a white horse (Rev. 6:2)? Doesn't that indicate that there will be animals in heaven?

Several Christian authors have weighed in on this question. Author and scholar Lee Strobel wrote the following:

> In response to this question, pet lovers tend to answer with a hearty, "Yes!" Indeed, the book of Revelation describes many creatures, some familiar and some fantastical, such as the four horses in Revelation 6:2–8. However, the Bible does not give a firm answer either way.
>
> Humans are the only creatures made in the image of God (see Genesis 1:26). Because of this, Adam and Eve's descendants have characteristics that members of the animal kingdom lack, such as a spiritual sensibility and the capacity to worship and love God. These unique qualities separate humans and animals in a significant way, suggesting that animals may not have souls that survive after death.
>
> However, the Bible says that, like humans (see Genesis 2:7), animals have "the breath of life" in them (Genesis 1:30; 6:17), which may indicate a soul of some type. Animals are also present in Isaiah's visionary description of the future consummation of the Messianic kingdom (see Isaiah 11:6–9).
>
> Ultimately, we cannot be sure whether or not animals will populate heaven. Evidence suggests that humans will receive different treatment in the afterlife than animals, yet that does not mean animals will be absent altogether.[53]

While Strobel does not come to a conclusion on the subject, author and teacher Hank Hanegraaff takes a more definitive view:

> Scripture does not conclusively tell us whether our pets will make it to heaven. However, the Bible does provide us with some significant clues regarding whether or not animals will

---

53. Lee Strobel, *The Case for Christ Study Bible* (Grand Rapids: Zondervan, 2010), Revelation 6:1–8.

inhabit the new heaven and the new earth. First, animals populated the Garden of Eden. Thus, there is a precedent for believing that animals will populate Eden Restored as well. Animals are among God's most creative creations. Thus, it would seem incredible that he would banish such wonders in heaven.

Furthermore, while we cannot say for certain that the pets we enjoy today will be "resurrected" in eternity, I am not willing to preclude the possibility. Some of the keenest thinkers from C. S. Lewis to Peter Kreeft are not only convinced that animals in general but that pets in particular will be restored in the resurrection. If God resurrected our pets it would be in total keeping with His overwhelming grace and goodness.

Finally, the Scriptures from first to last suggest that animals have souls. Both Moses in Genesis and John in Revelation communicate that the Creator endowed animals with souls. In the original languages of Genesis 1:20 and Revelation 8:9, [the words] *nephesh* and *psyche* respectively refer to the essence of life or soul. Not until . . . the Enlightenment did people think otherwise about animals. However, because the soul of an animal is qualitatively different from the soul of a human there is reasonable doubt that it can survive the death of its body. One thing is certain: Scripture provides us with sufficient precedence for believing that animals will inhabit the new heaven and new earth. In the words of Isaiah: "The wolf will live with the lamb, the leopard will lie down with the goat, the calf and the lion and the yearling together; and a little child will lead them" (Isaiah 11:6).[54]

---

54. Hank Hanegraaff, *The Bible Answer Book* (Nashville: Thomas Nelson, 2004), 135–136.

Will Squeaky make it to heaven? I don't know. But I am fairly certain that our heavenly home will include animals. I can just see it now: pet parakeets landing on my friends' shoulders, dogs playing fetch, and people riding their pet giraffes.

FOR FURTHER THOUGHT

What value do animals and pets bring to your life here on earth? Do you think your first pet will be waiting for you in heaven?

WHAT ARE THE ANGELS IN HEAVEN LIKE?

> Praise him, all his angels;
>   praise him, all his heavenly hosts.

—PSALM 148:2

When my wife and I were first married, we didn't own a TV, partly by choice and partly because we couldn't afford one. From time to time we would borrow a TV from church that picked up a few channels with its small antenna. It was during that time that we discovered a show on TV called *Touched by an Angel*. The angels were played by two ordinary-looking women. So is that what angels in heaven will be like, just like humans? Nothing extraordinary or different about them?

John MacArthur wrote this:

> Angels are . . . beings with all the attributes of personality: intellect, feelings, and volition. They have personalities. . . .

Angels are almost always portrayed in Scripture as highly intelligent beings. In Matthew 28:5, when the two Marys found Jesus' tomb empty on the morning of the resurrection, "The angel answered and said unto the women, Fear not ye: for I *know* that ye seek Jesus, which was crucified". . . . The angels communicate. They have conversations. They know things. They obviously are creatures of intellect.

Angels are not omniscient, however. First Peter 1:12 says the gospel contains truths that "the angels desire to look into." So there are some things they do not understand. Yet even their desire to know more proves that they are intelligent beings.

Angels also express emotion. Remember that they sang together at creation (Job 38:7). Luke 15:10 says "There is joy in the presence of the angels of God over one sinner that repenteth." I believe that verse speaks of *God's* joy over the salvation of His elect. But there is a sense in which that joy is also shared by angels. The parable Jesus tells in this context describes a woman who has lost a coin. She sweeps the house, takes a candle, and looks everywhere until she finds it. Then "she calleth her friends and her neighbours together, saying, Rejoice with me; for I have found the piece which I had lost" (v. 9). Then verse 10 says, "*Likewise*" there is joy over the salvation of a sinner. This clearly implies that God rejoices in the angels' presence so that they may share His joy! . . .

Look at Isaiah's description of angelic worship around the throne of God:

> *I saw also the Lord sitting upon a throne, high and lifted up, and his train filled the temple. Above it stood the seraphim: each one had six wings; with twain he covered his face, and with twain he covered*

*his feet, and with twain he did fly. And one cried
unto another, and said, Holy, holy, holy, is the Lord
of hosts: the whole earth is full of his glory.*

—ISA. 6:1–3

Isaiah's description of these majestic creatures makes
clear that they are not mere machines, or animals, but both
highly intelligent and capable of the profoundest emotions
associated with the highest kind of worship. It is also evident
that they have a will. Lucifer's sin was a willful pride. He said
in his heart, "I will ascend into heaven, I will exalt my throne
above the stars of God: I will sit also upon the mount of the
congregation, in the sides of the north: I will ascend above
the heights of the clouds; I will be like the most High" (Isa.
14:13–14). . . .

God Himself appeals to the wills of the angels. Hebrews
1:6 records God the Father's command to the angels at the
birth of His son: "And let all the angels of God worship
him." Obedience to any command involves an act of the
will. Not only do angels have all the attributes of personality, but they are also lofty creatures, slightly higher in
majesty and authority than humans. When Christ became
a man, Scripture says He was made "a little lower than the
angels" (Heb. 2:7). So angels occupy a higher state than we
do—at least for the time being. Someday redeemed humanity will judge the angels—and this may imply that we will
also rule over them in heaven. Paul wrote, "Know ye not
that we shall judge angels? How much more things that per-
tain to this life?" (1 Cor. 6:3). Jesus promised the churches
of Asia Minor, "To him that overcometh will I grant to sit
with me in my throne, even as I also overcame, and am set
down with my Father in his throne" (Rev. 3:21). Sharing the

> The Bible describes angels quite differently from how we see them on TV and in the movies.

throne of Christ may imply that we will have rule over the angels. If so, this is a stunning concept.[55]

In the Bible, whenever humans met angels they were always tempted to fall down and worship them because they were so spectacular in appearance. The Bible describes angels quite differently from how we see them on TV and in the movies. When we meet our first angel in heaven, I think we'll be pleasantly shocked and surprised.

FOR FURTHER THOUGHT

Read through the last book of the Bible, Revelation, and pay special attention to the descriptions of angels. How do those descriptions inspire you?

---

55. Taken from *The Glory of Heaven* by John MacArthur, © 1996, pp. 156–158. Used by permission of Crossway, a publishing ministry of Good News Publishers, Wheaton, IL 60187, www.crossway.org.

DOES EVERYONE GO TO HEAVEN EVENTUALLY?

> But our citizenship is in heaven. And we eagerly await a Savior from there, the Lord Jesus Christ.
>
> **—PHILIPPIANS 3:20**

"Trophies? What are these for?" I asked the league commissioner for my seven-year-old son's soccer league. We had just finished a season in which we lost almost every game. The commissioner told me that all the boys received the same trophies no matter how their team did. I bit my tongue and handed out the trophies after the final loss of the season. About ten years later, my son, recounting that moment, said, "I never understood why we got those trophies. We sure didn't deserve them."

Are our spiritual destinies like those golden trophies? Will everyone eventually receive a reward no matter how they lived on earth, no matter what choices they made? Will everyone go to heaven eventually?

Here's how best-selling author and pastor Francis Chan and coauthor Preston Sprinkle answered that question:

> [Philippians 2 says] Therefore God has highly exalted him and bestowed on him the name that is above every name, so that at the name of Jesus every knee should bow, in heaven and on earth and under the earth, and every tongue confess that Jesus Christ is Lord, to the glory of God the Father.
>
> The key phrase here is "every knee should bow . . . and every tongue confess that Jesus Christ is Lord" (vv. 10–11).

By itself, this could mean that every single individual who ever lived will embrace Jesus—if not in this life, then surely in the next.

But all we would need is for the rest of the Philippian letter to float ashore in order to see that Philippians 2:9–11 doesn't teach universal salvation. In Philippians 1:28, Paul says that those who oppose the gospel will face "destruction," while those who embrace it will be saved. There's a contrast here between believers and unbelievers; each have very different destinies. In Philippians 3:19, Paul refers to the enemies of Christ whose "end is destruction," while followers of Jesus look forward to resurrection and glory (3:20–21). Once more, there's a contrast. A contrast between believers and unbelievers and their individual destinies (note the word *end* in 3:19), which follow the decisions they make in this life.

We also need to see that Paul in Philippians 2 is actually quoting from the Old Testament book of Isaiah. Here, the prophet Isaiah looks forward to a time when every knee will bow and every tongue will confess the name of God (45:23). But in that passage, Isaiah is referring to God's salvation, which is *witnessed* among the nations and embraced by *some* but not all. In fact, Isaiah himself, in the very passage that Paul quotes, says that there will be some who embrace salvation and some who continue to resist it.[56]

---

56. See Howard Marshall, "The New Testament Does Not Teach Universal Salvation," in Robin A. Parry and Christopher H. Partridge, *Universal Salvation?: The Current Debate* (Grand Rapids: Eerdmans, 2004), 68–69. This reading is supported by the conclusion of the book of Isaiah, which depicts two groups of people, those on God's side and those who remain against Him: "[A]ll flesh shall come to worship before me, declares the Lord. And they shall go out and look on the dead bodies of the men who have rebelled against me. For their worm shall not die, their fire shall not be quenched, and they shall be an abhorrence to all flesh" (66:23–24). And that's how Isaiah ends. There will be restoration for those who turn to God, and judgment followed by punishment for those who don't.

So what does Philippians 2:9–11 mean? It means that there will come a day when Christ returns to reclaim His creation, and *everyone will acknowledge this*. King Jesus will reign, and none will be able to deny it. But Paul doesn't contradict Isaiah.[57] With this salvation and reign also comes judgment for those who opposed Christ in this life. Isaiah said this in the very next verse (45:24), and Paul affirms it as well (Phil. 1:28; 3:19).

Several passages in the New Testament describe God restoring all people or reconciling all things to Himself. These verses are often used to prove that God will save every single person.[58] Here are a few of the big ones:

> For as in Adam all die, so also in Christ shall all be made alive. (1 Cor. 15:22)

> In Christ God was reconciling the world to himself, not counting their trespasses against them, and entrusting to us the message of reconciliation. (2 Cor. 5:19)

> In him all the fullness of God was pleased to dwell, and through him to reconcile to himself all things, whether on earth or in heaven, making peace by the blood of his cross. (Col. 1:19–20)

---

57. Throughout Isaiah 40–66, the nations will "see" (40:5; 52:10, 15), "understand" (52:15) and even "know" about (45:6; 49:26) God's salvation of His people, but this doesn't mean that they embrace it. For instance, Isaiah says that the pagan king Cyrus the Great will "know that it is . . . the LORD" who raised him up, and yet the next verse says "though you do not know me" (Isa. 45:3–4). So does Cyrus "know" God or not? Yes and no. He knows God in the sense that he acknowledges God's sovereignty, but he doesn't know God so as to believe in Him for salvation. Now, to be sure, there will be many among the nations (i.e., Gentiles) who will embrace this God of Israel. This is an important theme in Isaiah as well (44:5; 45:14, 20–25; 49:7; 55:5). But Isaiah never says that everyone without exception will be saved.

58. Passages include Romans 5:18–19, Romans 11:32, and Ephesians 1:10.

> With this salvation and reign also comes judgment for those who opposed Christ in this life.

> [God] desires all people to be saved and to come to the knowledge of the truth. (1 Tim. 2:4)

In looking at these passages, one Christian Universalist says, "Paul envisioned a time when all persons would be reconciled to God in the full redemptive sense."[59]

Is that what these passages are saying, or is there something else going on?

There seems to be something else going on in 1 Corinthians 15:22, for instance, where Paul says, "In Christ all will be made alive" (NIV). The verse by itself could mean that everyone will end up being saved, but the context doesn't support this interpretation. When Paul says "all will be made alive," he's clearly thinking about the resurrection of *believers* at the second coming of Christ. In fact, he says this very thing in the next verse: "All who belong to Christ will be made alive at his coming" (see vv. 22–23).[60] So the verse can't mean that everyone will be saved in the end. . . .

So "all" doesn't always mean everything or everyone. And the same goes for 1 Corinthians 15:22, as is clear from

---

59. Thomas Talbott, "Christ Victorious," in Parry and Partridge, *Universal Salvation*, 25. Similarly, Rob Bell says "no one can resist God's pursuit forever, because God's love will eventually melt even the hardest of hearts" (*Love Wins*, (Rob Bell, *Love Wins*. (New York: HarperOne, 2011), 108.) In this quote, Bell is thinking of Colossians 1 in particular.

60. I've switched the order of words in 15:22–23 for clarity, but the meaning I'm giving here is clear from the context.

the context. The "all" who will be "made alive" in Christ refers to believers of all types, not every single person.[61]

My son was right: losing soccer teams usually don't "deserve" golden trophies for their losing season. In contrast, we see from this reading that the outcome of each person's choices in life will not automatically result in the golden trophy of salvation. Scripture is clear that Jesus is "the gate" that leads to eternal life. Everyone who chooses to believe in him and put their trust in him will have life and have it to the full (see John 10). Who do you say that Jesus is?

FOR FURTHER THOUGHT

Would it be fair for God to give a reward to those who wanted nothing to do with him during their lives on earth?

---

61. Francis Chan and Preston Sprinkle, *Erasing Hell: What God Said about Eternity, and the Things We've Made Up* (Colorado Springs: David C. Cook, 2011), 30. Used by permission.

LOOKING FORWARD
TO HEAVEN

J. Augustus Knapp; *Ceres Pleading Before Hades for the Liberation of Persephone*; early 20th c.

"Ask yourself whether the dream of heaven and greatness should be waiting for us in our graves—or whether it should be ours here and now and on this earth."

—Ayn Rand

"If you want to be perfect, go, sell your possessions and give to the poor, and you will have treasure in heaven."

—Jesus Christ (Matt. 19:21)

"Heaven is under our feet as well as over our heads."

—Henry David Thoreau

"On earth there is no heaven, but there are pieces of it."

—Jules Renard

"The best remedy for those who are afraid, lonely or unhappy is to go outside, somewhere where they can be quite alone with the heavens, nature and God. Because only then does one feel that all is as it should be and that God wishes to see people happy, amidst the simple beauty of nature. As long as this exists, and it certainly always will, I know that then there will always be comfort for every sorrow, whatever the circumstances may be. And I firmly believe that nature brings solace in all troubles."

—Anne Frank, *The Diary of a Young Girl*

"[To have faith in Christ] means, of course, trying to do all that He says. There would be no sense in saying you trusted a person if you would not take his advice. Thus if you have really handed yourself over to Him, it must follow that you are trying to obey Him. But trying in a new way, a less worried way. Not doing these things in order to be saved, but because He has begun to save you already. Not hoping to get to Heaven as a reward for your actions, but inevitably wanting to act in a certain way because a first faint gleam of Heaven is already inside you."

—C. S. Lewis, *Mere Christianity*

"The world's bumper sticker reads: Life sucks, and then you die. Perhaps Christian bumper stickers should read: Life sucks, but then you find hope and you can't wait to die."

—Ted Dekker, *The Slumber of Christianity: Awakening a Passion for Heaven on Earth*

The Lord is my light and my salvation—
whom shall I fear?
The Lord is the stronghold of my life—
of whom shall I be afraid?
When the wicked advance against me
to devour me,
it is my enemies and my foes
who will stumble and fall.
Though an army besiege me,
my heart will not fear;
though war break out against me,
even then I will be confident.
One thing I ask from the Lord,
this only do I seek:
that I may dwell in the house of the Lord
all the days of my life,
to gaze on the beauty of the Lord
and to seek him in his temple.
For in the day of trouble
he will keep me safe in his dwelling;
he will hide me in the shelter of his sacred tent
and set me high upon a rock.
Then my head will be exalted
above the enemies who surround me;
at his sacred tent I will sacrifice with shouts of joy;
I will sing and make music to the Lord.
Hear my voice when I call, Lord;
be merciful to me and answer me.

My heart says of you, "Seek his face!"
    *Your face, L*ORD*, I will seek.*
Do not hide your face from me,
    do not turn your servant away in anger;
    you have been my helper.
Do not reject me or forsake me,
    God my Savior.
Though my father and mother forsake me,
    *the L*ORD *will receive me.*
*Teach me your way, L*ORD*;*
    lead me in a straight path
    because of my oppressors.
Do not turn me over to the desire of my foes,
    for false witnesses rise up against me,
    spouting malicious accusations.
I remain confident of this:
    *I will see the goodness of the L*ORD
    in the land of the living.
*Wait for the L*ORD*;*
    be strong and take heart
    *and wait for the L*ORD*.*

—PSALM 27:1–14

HOW CAN WE VIEW DEATH AS A GOOD THING?

For to me, to live is Christ and to die is gain.

—PHILIPPIANS 1:21

Have you ever considered that death is not a loss but a gain? I know, it seems illogical and it contradicts what the world teaches, but it's true. Paul, one of the greatest Christian missionaries of all time, was often in prison because he went around preaching about Jesus, which made people angry. One of my favorite Bible verses comes from a letter Paul wrote from prison: "For to me, to live is Christ and to die is gain" (Phil. 1:21).

In his book *Heaven Revealed*, pastor and author Paul Enns explained more about why Paul could make such a statement:

> Paul had no fear of death. It didn't matter to Paul whether he lived or died. If he was living, it meant living in fellowship and service for Christ; if he died, it was advantageous. Paul made the startling statement, "To die is gain" (Phil. 1:21). How is death "gain"? "Gain" speaks of "advantage" and "profit . . . Paul says that for him to live is Christ, and therefore death, in which this life finds fulfillment in sight, is advantage or gain."[62] In what way? For Paul, death "could not in any way separate him from Christ (see Rom. 8:38–39). . . . [I]n death there was a continuing relationship with

---

62. Heinrich Schlier, "kerdos," in *Theological Dictionary of the New Testament*, ed. Gerhard Kittel and Gerhard Friedrich, vol. 5 (Grand Rapids: Eerdmans, 1967), 672–73.

Christ. Life which is centered on Christ is thus not destroyed by death; it is only increased and enriched by death."[63]

Death prevents us from staying in this sinful, suffering world of sickness. Erwin Lutzer reminds us that "only death can give us the gift of eternity. . . . Death [escorts us] into the presence of God. . . . Death might temporarily take our friends from us, but only to introduce us to that land in which there are no good-byes."[64]

What a wonderful, blessed truth. The believer living in fellowship with Christ transitions into a better, fuller, more wonderful relationship with Christ. The relationship is never separated; it is enhanced. It reminds me of an occasion when, as a young pastor, I spoke to an elderly, godly man from California, who, with his wife, visited the church I pastored. When I saw him alone, I asked him about his wife. He exclaimed, "Oh, she has gone home to be with the Lord. And I am so happy for her, that she is in the presence of Jesus, that I almost feel guilty that I'm not sorrowing more!"

I was startled at the man's response, but he had the biblical perspective. At death the believer enters into a fuller, more wonderful relationship with Christ. . . .

Paul says, "For we know that if the earthly tent which is our house is torn down, we have a building from God, a house not made with hands, eternal in the heavens" (2 Cor. 5:1). When we depart this earth for heaven, we leave behind our temporary dwelling and receive our permanent dwelling, "a building from God, a house not made with hands." The "house" describes "the glorified body of the departed Christian," note Gingrich and Danker.[65] "The earthly body is

63. Gerald F. Hawthorne, "Philippians" in *Word Biblical Commentary* (Waco, TX: Word, 1983), 46.

64. Erwin W. Lutzer, *One Minute After You Die* (Chicago: Moody, 1997), 45.

65. Gingrich and Danker, *A Greek-English Lexicon*, 559.

a tent which can be dismantled. . . . But then we have a house from God which is not made with hands, which is eternal, and which is ready in heaven."[66] The fact that the same root word *oikos* ("house") is used for both the body in this life and the new body in heaven is a reminder that immediately upon death the believer receives a greater body than he now possesses; even though it is prior to the resurrection when we will receive a glorified body.

The tent is a reminder that we are on a pilgrimage, like visiting a foreign country. A tent is temporary. After a brief sojourn on earth, we pull up stakes and trade in our tent for a heavenly home. We weren't made to live in a tent forever; we were made for a mansion.[67]

I'm often inspired by Paul's boldness and courage. He lived and breathed for Christ. He didn't fear death because he knew it would bring him fully into God's presence. I think this is why Paul could face being beaten, almost stoned to death, and imprisoned over and over. He knew something better awaited him.

FOR FURTHER THOUGHT

How can you live more fully for Christ today, knowing that death will only bring you closer to him?

---

66. Otto Michel, "oikos" in *Theological Dictionary of the New Testament*, ed. Gerhard Kittel and Gerhard Friedrich, vol. 5 (Grand Rapids: Eerdmans, 1967), 146.

67. Paul P. Enns, *Heaven Revealed: What Is It Like? What Will We Do? . . . And 11 Other Things You've Wondered About* (Chicago: Moody Publishers, 2011), 35–38.

WILL MY **PAST** FOLLOW ME INTO **HEAVEN?**

> No longer will there be any curse. The throne of God and of the Lamb will be in the city, and his servants will serve him.
>
> **—REVELATION 22:3**

Who doesn't have regrets? I sure have my share. I regret things I've said and things I didn't say. I regret things I've done and things I've been too afraid to do. Regret seems to be part of the common human experience. People often say, "The past is the past and should stay there," but is that possible? Our experiences have shaped who we are today. So when it comes to heaven, will our past follow us there too?

Dave Earley wrote the following explanation:

One major element that will make Heaven "heavenly" is that the curse of sin will be left far behind (Revelation 22:3). The transformational power of Jesus' death, burial, and resurrection for our sin will be experienced on a much greater level than we can now comprehend. Sin's penalty will be paid, its power broken, and its presence completely removed. There is no sin in Heaven.

Sin is breaking God's law. In Heaven there is no sin (Romans 6:14). Therefore, no one will break the law. In other words, there will be no bad people in Heaven (Revelation 21:8, 22:15). No one will steal, rob, rape, or murder. You will not need to fear being abused, molested, assaulted, mugged, or kidnapped. You won't have to lock the doors when you leave. Security systems and fences will be unnecessary. No one will need to carry a gun. Mace and pepper spray will be missing.

Sin is missing God's mark. In Heaven moral, spiritual, mental, emotional, and physical potential will be realized. Instead of focusing on illness and disease, health care persons can help us maximize health and nutrition. There will be no disease. There are no negatives in Heaven. . . .

I am quite certain that there will be "sinners" in Heaven—after all, I plan on being there. In fact, Heaven will be full of "sinners," or, more accurately, "*ex*-sinners." Former thieves, liars, murderers, and adulterers will abound. Didn't Jesus tell the thief on the cross he would join Jesus in Paradise (Luke 23:43)? Didn't Paul describe himself as the worst of sinners (1 Timothy 1:15)?

The human luminaries in Heaven will be a "who's who" of people with a past. Moses *was* a murderer. So *was* David. Joshua *had been* cowardly and initially lacked faith. So *did* Gideon, Moses, and Thomas. Rahab *was* a harlot. Bathsheba *was* an adulteress. Judah and David *were* adulterers. Mary Magdalene *had been* a very "loose woman." Solomon *had* three hundred concubines. He also *had* married hundreds of pagan women who turned his heart from the Lord.

Abraham and Jacob *had* terrible troubles with lying. Noah *had* a drinking problem. Miriam *was* a gossip. Jonah *ran* from God. Martha *was* a work-addicted worrier. Mary *might have been* a bit lazy. James and John *wrestled* with selfish ambition. Peter *denied* Jesus. The disciples *hid*. Mark *was* a quitter.

Every human in Heaven will have a past as a "sinner." All will be an ex-something (replace *something* with words like "liar," "drunk," "thief," "cheat," "gossip," "doubter," "glutton"). But, unlike people now on Earth, that sinful part of our personality will be gone, washed away forever by the power of the crucified blood of the Lord Jesus Christ. Our personalities will be transformed into what they were originally intended to be before the world, the flesh, and the devil twisted them into something hideous and grotesquely evil. They will be a glorious reflection of the character of the Lord Jesus. So, even though there will be "sinners" in Heaven, we will become gloriously transformed saints.

Heaven will be a much better place. You will like yourself and others much better because all our sinful tendencies will be gone.

One of the big reasons I committed my life completely to following Jesus Christ is because a long time ago I realized that I could never escape "me." I have to be with "me" 24/7. There is no place I can go on this planet to flee from myself. Therefore, I had better enjoy the person I am becoming. Other people will not always like me, but I had better be able to appreciate and respect the person I am.

One of the aspects of Heaven I am most thrilled about is I'll be the very best "me" I can be. Self-centeredness, selfish ambition, and selfishness will no longer be enemies I must constantly fight. Fear, doubt, dread, worry, and anxiety will not limit me. Bitterness, resentment, and anger will not have to be continually rooted out of my heart. Greed, lust, jealousy, and envy won't try to capture my heart. . . .

Knowing that Heaven is a much better place than Earth makes me long for Heaven. It also gives me patience with the imperfections of Earth, knowing that they will largely be forgotten in the superior perfections of Heaven.[68]

---

68. Dave Earley, *The 21 Most Amazing Truths About Heaven* (Uhrichsville, OH: Barbour Publishing, 2006), 46–47, 49.

So my past will be with me in heaven because it has shaped who I am. The big difference, though, is that it will no longer carry that sense of regret or guilt. My past will no longer have the power to make me behave in ways that are contrary to who God made me to be. In heaven we will be entirely new creations, finally stepping into the molds that God made for us when he knit us together in our mothers' wombs.

FOR FURTHER THOUGHT

What part of your past do you most regret? Do you long for the day when God redeems your past and makes you new?

WILL I BE ABLE TO FIND AND VISIT FRIENDS AND FAMILY MEMBERS IN HEAVEN?

"Let not your heart be troubled; you believe in God, believe also in Me. In My Father's house are many mansions; if it were not so, I would have told you. I go to prepare a place for you. And if I go and prepare a place for you, I will come again and receive you to Myself; that where I am, there you may be also."

JOHN 14:1–3

Bill Bright (founder of Campus Crusade for Christ) was an evangelist I greatly respected. While I never had the pleasure of meeting him personally, I heard him speak toward the end of his life on the topic of heaven. Watching him stand in front of an audience and preach while being fed oxygen through a tube near his nose was both inspiring and sobering.

As he spoke passionately about what the Bible taught about heaven, he also gave his listeners the sense—by his own admission—that he was going to be there soon. When I heard that he had passed away not too long after that sermon, I was reminded yet again about the brevity of life.

And while Dr. Bright was always someone I had admired, someone recently told me a story about him I had never heard before. The story goes that Dr. Bright was not only convinced of heaven but that he believed we would take our memories and friendships with us when we died. While talking with an aging friend, Bill recounted the warm feelings and memories they shared about a mutual friend who had died some time before. Bill said something like, "If you pass away before me, do me a favor. Look up our friend and tell him I said hello and that I'm looking forward to seeing him again."

I don't know if the story is true, but it makes sense to me. We have every indication that our memories, personalities, and friendships will indeed travel with us to heaven. Therefore, I suppose it is perfectly reasonable that we could ask someone to look up a friend and deliver a greeting.

S. Michael Houdmann of GotQuestions.org wrote the following:

> Many people say that the first thing they want to do when they arrive in heaven is see all their friends and loved ones who have passed on before them. In eternity, there will be plenty of time to see, know, and spend time with our friends and family members. However, that will not be our primary focus in heaven. We will be far more occupied with worshipping God and enjoying the wonders of heaven. Our reunions with loved ones are more likely to be filled with recounting the grace and glory of God in our lives, His wondrous love, and His mighty works. We will rejoice all the more because we can praise and worship the Lord in the company of other believers, especially those we loved on earth.

We have every indication that
our memories, personalities,
and friendships will indeed
travel with us to heaven.

What does the Bible say about whether we will be able to recognize people in the afterlife? King Saul recognized Samuel when the witch of Endor summoned Samuel from the realm of the dead (1 Samuel 20:8–17). When David's infant son died, David declared, "I will go to him, but he will not return to me" (2 Samuel 12:23). David assumed that he would be able to recognize his son in heaven, despite the fact that he died as a baby. In Luke 16:19–31, Abraham, Lazarus, and the rich man were all recognizable after death. At the transfiguration, Moses and Elijah were recognizable (Matthew 17:3–4). In these examples, the Bible does seem to indicate that we will be recognizable after death.

The Bible declares that when we arrive in heaven, we will "be like him [Jesus]; for we shall see him as he is" (1 John 3.2). Just as our earthly bodies were of the first man Adam, so will our resurrection bodies be just like Christ's (1 Corinthians 15:47). "And just as we have borne the likeness of the earthly man, so shall we bear the likeness of the man from heaven. For the perishable must clothe itself with the imperishable, and the mortal with immortality" (1 Corinthians 15:49,53). Many people recognized Jesus after His resurrection (John 20:16,20; 21:12; 1 Corinthians 15:4–7). If Jesus was recognizable in His glorified body, we also will be recognizable in our glorified bodies. Being able to see our loved ones is a glorious aspect of heaven, but heaven is far more about God, and far less about us. What a pleasure it will be to be reunited with our loved ones and worship God with them for all eternity.[69]

Wouldn't you like to find out if Bill's friend ever got the message? Here's an idea. When we get to heaven, let's look up Dr. Bright and ask him ourselves.

FOR FURTHER THOUGHT

Who would you like to greet in heaven?

WHAT GOOD IS IT TO THINK ABOUT HEAVEN WHILE STILL LIVING ON EARTH?

> But seek first his kingdom and his righteousness, and all these things will be given to you as well.
>
> **—MATTHEW 6:33**

Business guru and author Stephen Covey popularized the principle "Begin with the end in mind." That is solid advice for someone starting a business, for an artist selecting a canvas, or for an athlete who has dreams of a championship. The Christian life is no different. So, how can we remain focused on heaven

---

69. Houdmann, S. Michael. "Will We Be Able to See and Know Our Friends and Family Members in Heaven?" GotQuestions.org (http://www.gotquestions.org/family-heaven.html).

since it is our ultimate "end"? What does that look like practically, and how will that focus affect our time here on earth?

Bible teacher and author Wayne Martindale has interacted with a series of quotes from one of the most beloved Christian authors of all time, C. S. Lewis:

> We've all heard it: "Too heavenly minded to be of any earthly good." It is patently false. . . . This cliché gives Heaven a bad rap amongst earthlings. . . .
>
> The tension between living in the "City of Man" while journeying toward the "City of God" is as old as Abraham and is a major theme throughout the Bible and in writers as historically and theologically spread out as Augustine, Luther, and Richard Niebuhr.[70] As these writers affirm, nothing could be further from the truth than the notion that a person focused on Heaven has his head in the clouds and does nothing of practical value. If you are thinking of the heavenly streets of gold, so this line of thinking goes, you are likely to hit the potholes in the streets of Chicago. But history shows that the people most interested in the streets of gold are most likely to do something about the ones made of concrete and asphalt. Lewis points out, though he was not the first or last to do so, that it is precisely those who have the strongest belief in Heaven who have done the most earthly good. And this is quite apart from the fact that the best possible use of earthly time is to prepare for heavenly eternity. In *Mere Christianity*, Lewis says,

70. See, for example, St. Augustine, *The City of God* (London: Penguin, 1984); Martin Luther, "The Freedom of a Christian," in Luther's Works, Vol. 31; *Career of the Reformer*, ed. Harold J. Grimm (Philadelphia, PA: Muhlenberg Press, 1957), 327–377; and H. Richard Niebuhr, *Christ and Culture* (New York: Harper and Row, 1951).

Hope . . . means . . . a continual looking forward to the eternal. . . . It does not mean that we are to leave the present world as it is. If you read history you will find that the Christians who did most for the present world were just those who thought most of the next. . . . It is since Christians have largely ceased to think of the other world that they have become so ineffective in this. Aim at Heaven and you will get earth "thrown in": aim at earth and you will get neither.[71]

What contributions to earthly good have the heavenly minded made? In an essay entitled "Some Thoughts," Lewis tells us that Christianity is responsible for:

> [Preserving] such secular civilization as survived the fall of the Roman Empire . . . to it Europe owes the salvation, in those perilous ages, of civilized agriculture, architecture, laws, and literacy itself. . . . This religion has always been healing the sick and caring for the poor . . . it has, more than any other, blessed marriage . . . arts and philosophy tend to flourish in its neighbourhood.[72]

There are many reasons for this benevolence by Christians, but chief among them is the belief that God is the creator of all, and creation deserves respect because it is his. The human part of that creation, as something in his own image and something destined to live forever, demands our special regard. "Because we know the natural level also is God's creation we cannot cease to fight against the death which mars it, as against all those other blemishes upon it, against pain and poverty, barbarism and ignorance. Because we love

---

71. C. S. Lewis, *Mere Christianity* (New York: MacMillan, 1960), III.10:118.

72. C. S. Lewis, "Some Thoughts," *God in the Dock*, ed. Walter Hooper (Grand Rapids: Eerdmans, 1970), 147.

something else more than this world we love even this world better than those who know no other."[73, 74]

For Christians, keeping our minds and hearts in heaven often inspires earthly activity that brings the kingdom of God here and now. As Martindale wrote: "History shows that the people most interested in the streets of gold are most likely to do something about the ones made of concrete and asphalt."

FOR FURTHER THOUGHT

How might the idea of heaven inspire deeds of service and compassion in your life?

73. Ibid., 150.

74. Taken from *Beyond the Shadowlands: C.S. Lewis on Heaven and Hell* by Wayne Martindale, © 2005, pp. 46–47. Used by permission of Crossway, a publishing ministry of Good News Publishers, Wheaton, IL 60187, www.crossway.org.

DOES THE BIBLE OFFER ANY VISIONS OF HEAVEN?

In my vision at night I looked, and there before me was one like a son of man, coming with the clouds of heaven. He approached the Ancient of Days and was led into his presence. He was given authority, glory and sovereign power; all nations and peoples of every language worshiped him. His dominion is an everlasting dominion that will not pass away, and his kingdom is one that will never be destroyed.

—DANIEL 7:13–14

You can't go to a movie without seeing a number of commercials and previews before the featured presentation. While I could happily skip the pre-movie commercials and product placements, I do enjoy the sneak peeks about the movies coming out in the months ahead. Sometimes, on the drive home from the theater, my kids and I will talk more about the upcoming movies than about the movie we just watched. The anticipation of what's coming is simply exciting.

Throughout history, God has continued to give his people glimpses, or sneak peeks, into the heavenly realm. In the book of

Daniel in the Old Testament, Daniel recorded a powerful vision in which he saw someone like "the son of man." Daniel recorded this vision hundreds of years before Jesus came to earth. When he came, Jesus used the name "Son of Man" to describe himself more than any other name. In Daniel's visions, Daniel saw God the Father—the Ancient of Days—giving "the son of man" authority and power. He described a heavenly scene of worship and the coming of an indestructible kingdom.

Award-winning author Jonathan Aitken has explored other biblical visions of heaven:

> The Old Testament is a rich source of visionary traditions about heaven. Moses and the elders are reported in Exodus 24:11 to have ascended to the holy mountain where "they beheld God, ate and drank." The prophet Isaiah was admitted to the heavenly throne room full of seraphs and purified (Isaiah 6:1–8). His abject penitence during this beautifully described event, arguably the most powerful passage of theophany in the entire Bible, is a reminder that entry to heaven will be preceded by judgment. The same theme is suggested in the dreams of Daniel, who witnessed a heavenly scene of the judgment of wicked powers (Daniel 7).
>
> The Zion Psalms (Nos. 46, 48, 76, 87, 125, and 129) are full of pointers to what heaven could be like.
>
> Psalm 48 suggests that the city of God on his holy mountain is "beautiful in its loftiness, the joy of the whole earth." In the ensuing verses the psalmist portrays heaven as a fortress of absolute

The Book of Revelation is the classic document of the visionary tradition.

invincibility. Before its gates kings flee, strong men tremble, and mighty ships are shattered in the wind. This is a theological way of saying that man's power on earth offers no security whereas God's power in heaven gives total security.

The themes of feasting, joy, beauty, loftiness, and security also resonate in the visionary hints about heaven to be found in the New Testament. Its Greek word *ouranos* (literally sky or air) has derived into the English word heaven denoting the firmament above the earth where God has his abode. The first indication of this concept in the Gospels is to be found in Mark's account of the baptism of Jesus by John the Baptist in which the heavens open and a divine voice is heard saying, "This is my beloved son in whom I am well pleased" (Mark 1:10–11).

In Luke's Gospel, Jesus reports an experience in which he "watched Satan fall from heaven like a flash of lightning" (Luke 10:18). Jesus' vision has echoes of the Book of Revelation, whose author witnesses a heavenly war between the archangel Michael and the dragon who loses the war and is thrown down to earth, where he falls into a lake of fire (Revelation 12:9; 20:10). The Book of Revelation is the classic document of the visionary tradition. Its glimpses of heaven have been variously interpreted as literary fictions, visions of the early Christian seer John of Patmos, or experiences reported in the circle of John the Baptist and Jesus.

The visionary tradition is more subdued in the letters of Paul, but he describes in unambiguous terms how he experienced a heavenly journey and how he "was caught up to the third heaven. Whether it was in the body or out of the body I do not know—God knows" (2 Corinthians 12:3–4). In disclosing that he had this out of body experience 14 years earlier, Paul implied that heavenly visions are rare. John's Gospel also seems to emphasize the rarity of such experiences by stating that "no one has ascended into heaven except for the one who descended from heaven" (John 3:13).[75]

I think God knows that it's hard to wait for good things to come. Since he made us, he's familiar with our impatience and our temptation to give up before we reach our goals. God uses visions to inspire us, to keep us motivated to receive the fullness of all that he has for us. All these amazing visions of heaven are powerful previews of a full-length feature film to come.

FOR FURTHER THOUGHT

Can you think of an idea you've had that later became a reality?

 # HOW DOES LOOKING FORWARD TO HEAVEN AFFECT LIFE ON EARTH?

> For we were born only yesterday and know nothing,
>> and our days on earth are but a shadow.

—JOB 8:9

One of the most beloved songs in American church history, "Swing Low, Sweet Chariot," was written by the African American community during the dark years of enslavement. The song

---

75. Jonathan Aitken, "Heavenly Thoughts," *American Spectator.*

looks forward to the day when they would finally be carried out of slavery. The "home" to which they were carried is heaven, where freedom reigns: "Swing low, sweet chariot, coming for to carry me home."

I wonder how a hope for heaven changed how this community of people lived on earth while enduring suffering.

In *The Purpose Driven Life*, the best-selling nonfiction book in history, author and pastor Rick Warren tackled the question, "What on earth am I here for?"

> The Bible is full of metaphors that teach about the brief, temporary, transient nature of life on earth. Life is described as *a mist, a fast runner, a breath,* and *a wisp of smoke.* The Bible says, *"For we were born but yesterday. . . . Our days on earth are as transient as a shadow."*[76]
>
> To make the best use of your life, you must never forget two truths: First, compared with eternity, life is extremely brief. Second, earth is only a temporary residence. You won't be here long, so don't get too attached. Ask God to help you see life on earth as he sees it. David prayed, *"Lord, help me to realize how brief my time on earth will be. Help me to know that I am here for but a moment more."*[77]
>
> Repeatedly the Bible compares life on earth to temporarily living in a foreign country. This is not your permanent home or final destination. You're just passing through, just visiting earth. The Bible uses terms like *alien, pilgrim, foreigner, stranger, visitor,* and *traveler* to describe our brief stay on earth. David said, *"I am but a foreigner here on earth,"*[78]

---

76. Job 8:9 NLT.

77. Psalm 39:4 TLB.

78. Psalm 119:19 NLT.

We're not completely happy here because we're not supposed to be!

and Peter explained, *"If you call God your Father, live your time as temporary residents on earth."*[79]

In California, where I live, many people have moved from other parts of the world to work here, but they keep their citizenship with their home country. They are required to carry a visitor registration card (called a "green card"), which allows them to work here even though they aren't citizens. Christians should carry *spiritual* green cards to remind us that our citizenship is in heaven. God says his children are to think differently about life from the way unbelievers do. *"All they think about is this life here on earth. But we are citizens of heaven, where the Lord Jesus Christ lives."*[80] Real believers understand that there is far more to life than just the few years we live on this planet.

Your identity is in eternity, and your homeland is heaven. When you grasp this truth, you will stop worrying about "having it all" on earth. God is very blunt about the danger of living for the *here and now* and adopting the values, priorities, and lifestyles of the world around us. When we flirt with the temptations of this world, God calls it spiritual adultery. The Bible says, *"You're cheating on God. If all you want is your own way, flirting with the world every chance you get, you end up enemies of God and his way."*[81]

---

79. 1 Peter 1:17 GW.

80. Philippians 3:19–20 NLT.

81. James 4:4 MSG.

Imagine if you were asked by your country to be an ambassador to an enemy nation. You would probably have to learn a new language and adapt to some customs and cultural differences in order to be polite and to accomplish your mission. As an ambassador you would not be able to isolate yourself from the enemy. To fulfill your mission, you would have to have contact and relate to them.

But suppose you became so comfortable with this foreign country that you fell in love with it, preferring it to your homeland. Your loyalty and commitment would change. Your role as an ambassador would be compromised. Instead of representing your home country, you would start acting like the enemy. You'd be a traitor. . . .

The fact that earth is not our ultimate home explains why, as followers of Jesus, we experience difficulty, sorrow, and rejection in this world.[82] It also explains why some of God's promises seem unfulfilled, some prayers seem unanswered, and some circumstances seem unfair. This is not the end of the story.

In order to keep us from becoming too attached to earth, God allows us to feel a significant amount of discontent and dissatisfaction in life—longings that will *never* be fulfilled on this side of eternity. We're not completely happy here because we're not supposed to be! Earth is not our final home; we were created for something much better.[83]

I am inspired by the example set by the African American community that lived generations before me, enduring slavery and oppression. I hear in their music a hope for heaven and a faith that nothing in this world can take away. I wonder if it was

---

82. John 16:33; 16:20; 15:18–19.

83. Rick Warren, *The Purpose Driven Life: What on Earth Am I Here For?* (Grand Rapids: Zondervan, 2002), 47–50.

ultimately that hope for a heavenly home that birthed in them such beautiful music that praises a God who will one day set every captive free.

FOR FURTHER THOUGHT

Can you allow your hope for heaven to give you strength and endurance to face life's trials and challenges?

PART TWO

HELL

William Blake;
*The Thieves and
Serpents*, from *The
Divine Comedy*; 1827

THE REALITY OF HELL

HELL Canto 24

"One minute after we die, our minds, our memories, will be clearer than ever before."

—Erwin Lutzer

"It is not a question of God 'sending us' to hell. In each of us there is something growing, which will be hell unless it is nipped in the bud."

—C. S. Lewis

"I say let the world go to hell, but I should always have my tea."

—Fyodor Dostoyevsky

"I believe I am in Hell, therefore I am."

—Arthur Rimbaud

"Hell is truth known too late."

—J. C. Ryle

"My question must be—and is—not what does my heart tell me, but what does God's word say?"

—John Stott

Though you already know all this, I want to remind you that the Lord at one time delivered his people out of Egypt, but later destroyed those who did not believe. And the angels who did not keep their positions of authority but abandoned their proper dwelling—these he has kept in darkness, bound with everlasting chains for judgment on the great Day. In a similar way, Sodom and Gomorrah and the surrounding towns gave themselves up to sexual immorality and perversion. They serve as an example of those who suffer the punishment of eternal fire.

—JUDE vv. 5–7

 ## DOES HELL **EXIST?**

> But how then would the
> Scriptures be fulfilled that say it
> must happen in this way?
> **—MATTHEW 26:54**

The fact that hell is a very real place is not an easy issue to think or talk about. I would prefer it didn't exist and that everyone could enjoy heaven. My preference is irrelevant, because the Bible is clear on the topic. So, how can we make sense of it? I find comfort in the fact that I'm not alone in grappling with this subject. Some of the greatest Christian thinkers in the past and the present have wrestled with questions about hell's existence. After all, if hell exists, what does that say about God? Why would a loving God create such a place? Dr. Paul Copan, a well-respected professor at Palm Beach Atlantic University, said this:

> If God has broken into the world and spoken through Christ, then there are going to be certain beliefs that we're going to have to accept. It's not up to us to say, "I like this; I don't like that." C. S. Lewis said he'd gladly get rid of the doctrine of hell, but he concluded he couldn't, because there are certain things that flow from the claims of Christ and the teachings of the New Testament that precluded him from doing so. There needs to be that kind of honesty.
>
> We can certainly admit that we find certain doctrines troubling. But to pick and choose which doctrines we accept is to deny the teachings of Jesus, who through his resurrection has demonstrated the reliability of his claim of being the Son of God.
>
> Look at it this way: We may have subjective preferences about what doctrines we like and don't like. However, those subjective preferences can't change the objective reality that Jesus is God's unique revelation to humankind. If we want to sync up with reality, we need to sync up with him. We can't change reality just by refusing to believe certain doctrines that Jesus affirms. We may not like the doctrine of hell, but that can't change the objective reality of whether or not hell exists. We can't wish it out of existence. It either exists, as Jesus affirms, or it doesn't.[84]

Dr. J. P. Moreland is a scholar and philosopher who teaches at Talbot School of Theology and Biola University. He added this:

> Passages of Scripture such as 2 Peter 2:4–9 can raise many questions for people. For instance, you may be asking

---

84. Lee Strobel, *The Case for Christ Study Bible* (Grand Rapids: Zondervan, 2010).

yourself, "Do I buy into the concept of hell or not?" If you're only factoring into your deliberation the pros and cons of hell by itself, then you may be missing the point. After all, there's a lot of other evidence that you should consider that has nothing to do with hell per se, but which is relevant nonetheless. What evidence? It's all the evidence that there's a God, that he created you, that the New Testament is historically trustworthy, that Jesus performed miracles and rose from the dead, that God wants to spend eternity with you in heaven.

When you factor all of that in, you might say to yourself, "Even though I might not have a completely good explanation at this point for why there's a hell, I know there's got to be one because I have too much evidence that Jesus Christ really is the Son of God and he taught about it. And because I can trust him and his deep love for people—as demonstrated by his death for us on the cross—I can have confidence that hell will eventually make sense, that I'll see its fairness and that I will ultimately recognize it as being the best moral alternative."[85]

The doctrine of hell can understandably be a stumbling block to spiritual seekers. Dr. J. P. Moreland responded this way:

Whenever you're trying to start a friendship with any person, you don't understand everything about him and you don't necessarily agree or feel good about every view he holds. But you have to ask, on balance, do you trust this

---

85. J. P. Moreland as quoted in *The Case for Christ Study Bible*, Note at 2 Peter 2:4, 9.

person enough to want to enter a friendship with him? The same is true with Jesus. Every single issue isn't going to be resolved before we enter into a relationship with him. But the question is, on balance, can you trust him? I'd encourage any seeker to read the Gospel of John and then ask, "Can I trust Jesus?" I think the answer is yes. And I believe that, over time, as we develop our relationship with him, we'll even come to trust him in those areas where right now we lack complete understanding.[86]

One thing I do know is this: God is full of mystery and goodness. I don't always understand why he does the things he does. I readily admit that my limited human brain cannot fully understand the depth of God and the concept of eternity. Even so, wrestling with these topics is good. Each time I do, I am able to understand God and his plan a little better.

FOR FURTHER THOUGHT

What are some things that keep you from believing in God's goodness?

---

86. J. P. Moreland as quoted in *The Case for Christ Study Bible*, Note at Jude vv. 5–7.

IS HELL **REAL** OR JUST A **SCARE** TACTIC USED BY JESUS?

> If your hand or your foot causes you to stumble, cut it off and throw it away. It is better for you to enter life maimed or crippled than to have two hands or two feet and be thrown into eternal fire. And if your eye causes you to stumble, gouge it out and throw it away. It is better for you to enter life with one eye than to have two eyes and be thrown into the fire of hell.
>
> **—MATTHEW 18:8–9**

Have you ever exaggerated when you wanted to make a point? Ever embellished a story to make it more exciting? Some people say that Jesus used hyperbole or exaggeration when he spoke, in order to make a strong point. So when Jesus was teaching about hell, was he exaggerating or is it really as bad as he said it is?

I've always enjoyed listening to Dr. Tony Evans preach. On this topic, he said:

> Thinking seriously and biblically about hell is not something most people do. But Christians need to understand what God has saved them from, and unbelievers need to be warned of the eternal judgment that awaits them unless they repent of their sins and turn to Christ for salvation.

I know it's not popular to talk about hell. It's not surprising that in one survey, 76 percent of the people polled believed in heaven, while only 6 percent believed in hell. But my goal is to be biblical, not popular. A lot of people cope with the idea of hell by denying its reality. Some would argue that hell is a leftover superstition from the Dark Ages and that we are too enlightened in the twenty-first century to believe in such a medieval concept.

There are two other popular "coping mechanisms" that some people use to get around the Bible's clear teaching on hell. One is called annihilation, which teaches that unbelievers are not punished eternally after death, but are annihilated so that they simply cease to exist. Another belief that avoids having to deal with hell is the teaching of universalism. There are different forms of this, but the basic idea is that because God is good and loving He wouldn't condemn anyone to a place of eternal torment. So in the end everybody will be saved, even non-Christians, because all roads eventually lead to God and to heaven.

This issue is so important that we must allow God to speak for Himself through His Word. We must subject our concepts of hell to God's revelation. So let's see what the Bible says about what hell is really like. The first fact we need to establish is the undeniable reality of hell.

Let's start with a definition. Hell is the place of eternal exile where the ungodly will experience God's righteous retribution against sin forever. We are going to see that of all the suffering in hell, the worst is the fact that the lost are banished from God's presence forever. Jesus believed hell was a real place, and He taught its reality throughout His ministry. While teaching on the judgment awaiting the Gentiles, Jesus called hell "eternal fire" and "eternal punishment" (Matthew 25:41, 46).

These are just two of many verses in which the Bible clearly teaches the reality of hell as a place of punishment. Jesus said more about hell than He did about either heaven or love. So if the Lord's teaching on hell isn't trustworthy, if He was deceiving us on the reality of this place, how do we know we can trust Him when He tells us about heaven? This is the problem with those who try to pull out of the Bible only the parts they like, while denying the less pleasant parts. We can see the impossibility of this when we read the full text of Matthew 25:46. Jesus said concerning the unrighteous Gentiles being judged, "These will go away into eternal punishment, but the righteous into eternal life." The word for "eternal" is the same in both instances, which means Jesus was teaching that hell is just as eternal, and as real, as heaven. Jesus also characterized hell as a place of never-ending punishment, a clear message that we can't skip, ignore, or water down.

Jesus also taught in the most stark terms that hell is a place to be avoided at all costs. He said in Matthew 18:8–9 it would be better for us to cut off a hand or a foot, or put out an eye, than to be condemned to hell. Jesus wasn't teaching self-mutilation as a means of dealing with sin, because you can pluck out your eye and still be a lustful or envious person. He was telling us to do whatever it takes, no matter how radical, to rid our lives of sin, because sin can lead us into hell. It is better to lose some things in this life than to be lost for eternity in hell. Another reason I know hell is real is that death is real. Death only exists

Jesus also taught in the most stark terms that hell is a place to be avoided at all costs.

because of sin. If there were no sin, there would be no death. The presence of physical death is a testimony to us of the unseen, eternal reality of what the Bible calls the "second death" (Revelation 20:14), or hell. Trying to deny hell is as futile as trying to deny death. Hell is a reality that won't go away just because people don't want to think about it.[87]

Yes, Jesus used hyperbole when he told people to pluck out their eyes if their eyes caused them to sin; he wasn't really telling people to do that. He was exaggerating in order to make this point: "Get rid of sin and come to me! I am the only one who can keep you from the results of sin: death, destruction, and ultimately, hell." And though Jesus sometimes used hyperbole, there is no evidence that he used that literary device to exaggerate the dangers of hell. Instead, he repeatedly taught that hell is a reality that we will face if we choose to reject his words and his love.

FOR FURTHER THOUGHT

Is there a sin in your life that you need Jesus' strength and power to overcome?

---

87. Tony Evans, *Tony Evans Speaks Out on Heaven and Hell* (Chicago, IL: Moody Publishers, 2000), 11–14.

DO WE STILL NEED HELL TODAY?

> You made [human beings] rulers over
> the works of your hands;
> you put everything under their feet:
> all flocks and herds,
> and the animals of the wild.
>
> **—PSALM 8:6–7**

What separates humankind from the animals? From among many things, our ability to reason and to choose, to make decisions of the will. Every day, people choose between life and death, right and wrong, love and hate. You and I make moral choices.

The following excerpt contains a quote from the famous writer Flannery O'Connor: "No hell, no dignity." This statement intrigues me. What did she mean? How can a place of suffering bring dignity to humankind, separating us from the animals and the rest of creation?

Like the majority of Americans, I struggle to linger on the idea of hell. Most of us don't want to spend more than sixty seconds thinking about it. I know I'm not alone. In fact, someone once asked me, "Do we still need hell today? Or why can't we just make it go away?"

An article from *The Christian Century*, a popular publication, says:

A street preacher works a corner just blocks from the Christian Century office, loudly warning passersby of the wrath to come. It's always tempting to wonder, "If that is the Good News, what's the bad news?" Nevertheless, there is logic to this man's ministry. If he truly believes that most people are going to hell, then it makes sense for him to warn as many as possible.

A recent book by two Quaker ministers takes up the old issue of hell and who will go there. *If Grace Is True* (HarperSanFrancisco), by Philip Gulley and James Mulholland, is getting some attention, especially in evangelical circles. The authors make the case for the "universalist" position—that all will be saved—arguing that no one stands outside God's grace.

This is not a new instance in Christian thought. It's been a stream of Christian theology at least since Origen in the third century. "For the Almighty nothing is impossible, nor is anything beyond the reach of cure by its Maker," said Origen. And though half or more of the American people claim to believe in hell, most mainline Christians are implicitly if not explicitly universalists.

In addition to the argument for universal salvation based on the wideness of God's mercy, there is an argument on the basis of God's justice. Since no finite human can commit infinite sin, a sentence of infinite punishment just doesn't fit the crime.

Still, there's a problem in dispensing with hell entirely. If there is no hell—if God's grace is ultimately irresistible—then it would seem that humans lack true freedom. They can't decide against God. Further, the prospect of hell underscores the significance of our decisions and actions. Actions have consequences. As Flannery O'Connor put it, without hell humans would be like animals. "No hell, no dignity."

> God has made humans different
> from the animals in that we have
> a choice to love or reject him.

Since the Enlightenment, many Christians have been reluctant to say much about the "last things"—death, final judgment, heaven and hell—while other parts of the church talk about them with great specificity and assurance. Part of the challenge is that the biblical message on these topics is conveyed through figurative images that are ambiguous and sometimes contradictory. Therefore reverent agnosticism seems far preferable to the elaborate speculation found, for example, in the *Left Behind* series of novels.

Yet this much can be confessed: since God is the same yesterday, today and forever—as scripture attests of Jesus Christ—then God will be faithful in the future. That means that God will not force us to love him. It also means that God, like the father of the Prodigal Son, will never turn out the lights on us, will never assume that we are beyond redemption. That's a message worth taking to the streets.[88]

God has made humans different from the animals in that we have a choice to love or reject him. If you take away our free will, you take away our humanness. If you take away our humanness, you take away our ability to make moral choices and to love God and others. If hell does not exist, I am left to my own devices. I am left to be the god of my own universe, to decide what is

---

88. Copyright © 2003 by *The Christian Century.* "Do We Still Need Hell?" by Christian Century Editors is reprinted in excerpted form by permission from the October 4, 2003, issue of *The Christian Century.*

morally right or wrong. I don't know about you, but I don't want that responsibility. I'd rather let God make those decisions.

FOR FURTHER THOUGHT

Why do you think freedom is an essential ingredient in a loving relationship?

SHOULDN'T **HELL BE DOWNGRADED** TODAY?

> For all have sinned and fall short of the glory of God, and all are justified freely by his grace through the redemption that came by Christ Jesus.
>
> **—ROMANS 3:23–24**

Growing up on the East Coast, we had a routine for summer hurricane season. We'd hear the forecasts, watch the news of the storms hitting Florida, and then prepare the house. This routine worked for us. We never had really bad damage, in part because we were always prepared. Imagine how different the outcomes could have been had the broadcasters decided to downplay hurricanes, calling them heavy rainstorms instead.

I think it's important to call things by what they really are, don't you? If it's a hurricane, call it a hurricane, not a rainstorm. In the same way, I wonder how our lives would be affected if we stopped calling hell what it really is: hell. If we downgraded its name and intensity, how would that impact our daily lives and the good news of salvation?

Carol Zaleski, who teaches at Smith College, had one of her students ask her, "Shouldn't hell be downgraded from a hurricane to a tropical storm, from Gehenna to Sheol?" Here are her thoughts:

> From the gospel we have heard the absolute word of hope. We have heard that Christ conquered death and despoiled hell. We have seen the icons of Christ crushing hell's jaws; we have heard him call out to Adam, "Sleeper awake, I did not create you to be a prisoner of hell!" Why, then, a student once asked me, do Christians continue to believe in hell? Shouldn't hell be downgraded from a hurricane to a tropical storm, from Gehenna to Sheol?
>
> My first instinct was to agree. Child of my age, I find hell baffling and repugnant. I'm against capital punishment, against corporal discipline. Every motherly instinct tells me that children should be reared by hugs, not threats. If I held God to the same standard, I'd be a universalist or an annihilationist.
>
> Nonetheless, I had to tell my student that far from being abolished by the gospel, hell—eternal hell, with the undying worm and unquenchable fire—is a Christian distinctive.
>
> A look at the world's religions suggests, moreover, that it's a distinctive that makes a difference. Though few religious traditions have devised more nightmarish

Every motherly instinct tells me that children should be reared by hugs, not threats.

hells than Buddhism, Buddhist hells are as temporary as Buddhist heavens; one relapses from them into other births, until at last the stain of individuality dissolves. Nor are Buddhist hells like Christian purgatory; for the holy souls in purgatory are already sealed for heaven, experiencing, through their pains, a blessedness from which they cannot fall away.

Hence the Christian distinctive: individuality is for keeps. If there is a blessedness from which one cannot fall away, there is also a cursedness from which the truly depraved, who say no to blessedness with all their being, cannot be forced to depart. Christ has robbed death of its sting and deprived the devil of many a tasty meal, but hell persists, we are told, because freedom of the will requires it and justice demands it. It wasn't just "abandon hope" that Dante saw inscribed over the entrance of hell, but "justice moved my maker on high; divine power made me, wisdom supreme, and primal love."

There's no subject on which I'm more skeptical of my own—and our common—opinion. Of course we'd prefer to think that divine mercy will empty hell and set free every human captive, if not every last demon or imp. Of course we think ourselves well rid of the carking, soul-destroying guilt and judgmentalism that hell once evoked. But are we really serious? Abolish hell, and see how salvation dims down. Strike the "Inferno" from the Divine Comedy, and see how a blandness overtakes even "Purgatory" and "Paradise," turning the cosmic drama of sin and salvation into a spiritualist soap opera of inevitable progress. Abolish hell, and a host of smaller obsessions will fill the gap. For our fears we will always have with us, whether of hell or of comparative

> As you and I think about hell, may
> we have the courage to speak
> about it with both grace and truth.

trifles. Keep hell in view, and the trifles will fade as the promise of salvation burns bright.[89]

If weather reporters were more interested in making sure we felt good about our days rather than reporting the truth, we wouldn't be prepared for the coming hurricanes. Similarly, you and I have a job. It may not "feel good" to talk about hell, and it may not be the message others want to hear, but it is a necessary part of the news that we have to share with the world. As you and I think about hell, may we have the courage to speak about it with both grace and truth.

FOR FURTHER THOUGHT

Are there aspects of hell that you would like to downgrade or get rid of completely?

---

89. Copyright © 2003 by *The Christian Century*. "What to Say About Hell?" by Carol Zaleski is reprinted in excerpted form by permission from the June 3, 2008, issue of *The Christian Century*.

HOW SHOULD THE REALITY OF HELL MOTIVATE US TO ACT IN THIS WORLD?

> When he saw the crowds, he had compassion on them, because they were harassed and helpless, like sheep without a shepherd.
>
> **—MATTHEW 9:36**

I used to be a news junkie. Big time. Even as a kid I had a paper route and would read each issue after I finished my route. As an adult I would read the paper, browse news sites, and listen to news radio every day during my hour-long commute. Then one day last fall, I abruptly decided to snap the radio off, stop reading the paper, and delete my news bookmarks. I'd simply had enough—enough of the stories of murder, rape, and drive-by shootings. Enough of the stories of human suffering. These stories were, in a real way, hell's presence on earth and I was tired of filling my mind with them. As a follower of Christ, what should be my response to hell's "presence" in our world? I'm convinced that one of our jobs is to fight evil, overcome injustice, and bring aspects of heaven into this world.

John R. Franke, who teaches at Biblical Theological Seminary, and Leon Morris, a leading New Testament scholar who wrote many commentaries, shared these thoughts:

I have a vivid memory of an evangelistic event I attended as an undergraduate. The slick multimedia presentation of the gospel focused extensively on the torments of hell. At the conclusion, we were urged to trust in Jesus in order to escape this fiery fate. I was appalled. It was emotionally manipulative and designed to scare people into faith. The gospel was presented as little more than an escape from future agonies. From this perspective, it is hardly surprising that hell has fallen out of favor with many Christians.

However, in wrestling with this question over the years, I have come to think that in spite of the distortions of hell in some traditions, eradicating references to hell is shortsighted and has troubling consequences for the shape of our witness to the gospel. To be sure, there is much about Christian teaching on hell that is subject to critical scrutiny. But in its most basic form, it serves as a warning concerning the judgment of God against evil, injustice and callousness in the face of human need and brokenness. It is a reminder of the righteousness and justice of a God who stands over against the principalities and powers that are characterized by the oppression of others and indifference to their suffering. It bears witness to the hope that in due course God will put things right and evil will be justly condemned and vanquished.

The resources for recovering these aspects of Christian teaching on hell are close at hand, residing in the Gospels, which repeatedly portray Jesus speaking about judgment and hell. While the presence of these texts should work against the elimination of hell from the lexicon of Christian witness, the pressing question concerns the communication of this idea in the present cultural moment.

I suggest that we appropriate the idea of hell as a witness to the seriousness with which Jesus Christ enters into solidarity with those who are poor and disenfranchised. In the midst of the tournament of narratives that compete for allegiance in our society and in our souls, Jesus calls us to join him in his mission of proclaiming good news to the poor, setting the oppressed free and seeking those who are lost. We participate by providing food for the hungry, water for the thirsty, clothing for the naked, hospitality to the stranger, companionship to the imprisoned and comfort to the sick, and so enter into solidarity with Jesus himself.

Narratives that set themselves against the poor, the helpless, the oppressed and the marginalized are opposed to the mission of God in Jesus Christ. Christian teaching on hell reminds us that at the consummation of all things when the will of God is done on Earth as it is heaven, these inhumane narratives will be consigned to the "eternal fire," where they will be banished once and for all. What of those who have chosen to participate in them?[90]

Morris, in a separate article, added this:

We remember that Jesus wept over Jerusalem (Luke 19:41), and further that he counseled the "daughters of Jerusalem" to weep not for him, but for themselves and their children (Luke 23:28). And we recall that, while Paul could be certain that Israel would suffer for its rejection of Christ, he spoke of the "great sorrow and unceasing anguish" he had because of this. He went so far as to say, "For I could wish that I myself were accursed from Christ for my brothers' sake" (Rom. 9:2–3).

That is the authentic Christian approach. To accept the plain teaching of the New Testament about final retribution

---

90. Copyright © 2003 by *The Christian Century*. "What to Say About Hell?" by John Franke is reprinted in excerpted form by permission from the June 3, 2008, issue of *The Christian Century*.

> There will be a day when God
> will bring justice on earth.

does not result in complacency or in thinking oneself a cut above those who choose to
cut themselves off from God's salvation. It rather
means entering in some degree into the mind of
Christ. It means sorrow for those who are lost. It means
a firm determination to give ourselves over to such prayer
and promotion of evangelism that we will "by all means save
some" (1 Cor. 9:22).[91]

One day there will be no more need for the nightly news reporting on the day's acts of violence. There will be a day when God will bring justice on earth. This should motivate us, as Morris says, to not only pray for those who are lost, but to also share the gospel, the good news, that Jesus can change and save even the harshest sinner, from a murderer (Saul) into an evangelist (Paul). With God, nothing is impossible.

FOR FURTHER THOUGHT

Can you think of ways to adapt your language in order to talk to someone about Jesus in a way that they can understand?

---

91. Leon Morris, "The Dreadful Harvest," *Christianity Today* 35, no. 6: 34 (May 27, 1991). *Academic Search Premier,* EBSCO*host* (accessed August 14, 2013).

Unknown Artist;
A Soul Tormented in Hell (detail),
from *The Book of the Seven Mortal Sins*;
15th c.

HELL AS A CHOICE

"The safest road to hell is the gradual one—the gentle slope, soft underfoot, without sudden turnings, without milestones, without signposts."

—C. S. Lewis

"Then I saw that there was a way to hell, even from the gates of heaven."

—Paul Bunyan, *The Pilgrim's Progress*

"I'm on the highway to hell."

—AC/DC

"Hell has three gates: lust, anger, and greed."

—Indian proverb

"We are free to resist, reject, and rebel against God's ways for us. We can have all the hell we want."

—Rob Bell

"Everybody's got the right to go to hell in the handcart of their choice."

—Val McDermid

God "will repay each person according to what they have done." To those who by persistence in doing good seek glory, honor and immortality, he will give eternal life. But for those who are self-seeking and who reject the truth and follow evil, there will be wrath and anger.

—ROMANS 2:6–8

 # WHY DOES HELL EXIST? .

There will be trouble and distress for every human being who does evil: first for the Jew, then for the Gentile.

—ROMANS 2:9

Hell exists, ironically, because freedom exists. Does that sound confusing? Pope Benedict XVI remarked, "Today, society does not talk about hell. It's as if it did not exist, but it does. There is eternal punishment for those who sin and do not repent." He points out that hell exists because of sin and, ultimately, because there are people who will choose to reject the love of God. When they die, where will they go if they don't want to hang out with God forever?

Robert Yarbrough was a New Testament professor at Wheaton when I was a student there. He explained:

The tension between God's sovereignty and humanity's freedom is also evident in God's sending of guilty sinners to hell.

God's sovereignty is expressed in his judgment. This theme recurs a number of times in the Gospels and Revelation, and it shows that the power of God over the wicked extends beyond the grave. The Bible also indicates that God rules over hell. Unfortunately, some have erred at this point. As one writer said, "Hell is where Satan rules . . . where his complete fury is unleashed." But this is wrong, for hell is where God alone rules and where his fury is unleashed against Satan, his angels, and wicked human beings.

The book of Revelation also says that God chooses who will go to heaven—in fact, that he has enrolled their names "in the book of life from the creation of the world" (Rev. 17:8).[92]

A focus on God's sovereignty doesn't tell the whole story, however. Throughout the Bible, eternal judgment is most often traced to misused human freedom. Both the Old and New Testaments say that God will judge sinners according to their deeds:

> I will deal with them according to their conduct, and by their own standards I will judge them. Then they will know that I am the LORD. (Ezek. 7:27)

> The LORD Almighty has done to us what our ways and practices deserve, just as he determined to do. (Zech. 1:6)

> For the Son of Man is going to come . . . and then he will reward each person according to what they have done. (Matt. 16:27)

> Do not be deceived: God cannot be mocked. A man reaps what he sows. The one who sows to please his

---

92. John H. Gerstner, *Repent or Perish: With a Special Reference to the Conservative Attack on Hell* (Ligonier, PA: Soli Deo Gloria, 1990), 189–90.

sinful nature, from that nature will reap destruction. (Gal. 6:7–8)

Passage after passage points to a just God who gives sinners what they deserve. Those whose lives are characterized by evil thoughts, words, and deeds reap God's wrath. Why do people end up in hell? Scripture repeatedly blames human freedom used wrongly.

Revelation 20 captures both sides of the picture, showing how God's sovereignty and human freedom work together in determining who will go to hell.

> Then I saw a great white throne and him who was seated on it. The earth and the heavens fled from his presence, and there was no place for them. And I saw the dead, great and small, standing before the throne, and books were opened. Another book was opened, which is the book of life. The dead were judged according to what they had done as recorded in the books. The sea gave up the dead that were in it, and death and Hades gave up the dead that were in them, and each person was judged according to what they had done. Then death and Hades were thrown into the lake of fire. The lake of fire is the second death. Anyone whose name was not found written in the book of life was thrown into the lake of fire. (Rev. 20:11–15)

Summing it all up, Scripture presents God as the sovereign Judge before whom sinners stand on judgment day. They are condemned for abusing their human freedom in their rebellion against their Maker.[93]

---

93. Timothy Keller, R. Albert Mohler Jr., J. I. Packer, and Robert Yarbrough, *Is Hell for Real or Does Everyone Go to Heaven?* (Grand Rapids: Zondervan, 2011), 53–55.

So what will I do with my freedom to choose? The power to choose life or death, heaven or hell, is in my hands. That's a scary thought. But God loves us too much to force himself upon us, knowing coercion or manipulation is no love at all. Thankfully, I find God drawing me toward him with his goodness. He speaks tenderly to each of us, offering us the free gift of life through his Son, Jesus. What will we do with that gift?

FOR FURTHER THOUGHT
What will you do with your freedom to choose?

DOES GOD **BANISH PEOPLE** TO HELL OR DO THEY **CHOOSE** THAT **DESTINATION** THEMSELVES?

Keep yourselves in God's love as you wait for the mercy of our Lord Jesus Christ to bring you to eternal life.
—**JUDE** v. 21

Before the world of iPods and portable music devices, there was the boom box. People would walk through the city proudly sharing their music with a city block. While I never owned one, there was a high schooler on my junior high bus who always sat near me and cranked up his tunes. It was during those years that I was introduced to Metallica. I remember one song, "Master of

Puppets," that described people as puppets who were controlled by their "Master." According to the lyrics of the song, people were mastered, or enslaved, by their sins. It's an interesting idea. And while I didn't care for the song, it got me thinking: What truly controls me? Do I have the power to make choices in my life, the power to choose heaven or hell? Or does only God have that power?

Timothy Keller, best-selling author and pastor, explained the concept of slavery or sin in this way:

> I do not define sin as just breaking rules but also as "making something besides God our ultimate source of value and worth." These good things, which become idols, enslave us mentally and spiritually and drive us relentlessly, even to hell if we let them. . . .
>
> C. S. Lewis's imagining of hell can be helpful for secularists. In *The Great Divorce*, Lewis describes a busload of people from hell who come to the outskirts of heaven. In the story, they are urged to leave behind the sins that have trapped them in hell. Lewis's descriptions of people in hell are striking because they mirror the denial and self-delusion of substance abusers. When addicted to alcohol or an idol like success or money, we are miserable, but we blame others and pity ourselves; we do not take responsibility for our behavior or see the roots of our problem. Lewis writes:
>
>> Hell . . . begins with a grumbling mood, and yourself still distinct from it: perhaps even criticizing it. . . . You can repent and come out of it again. But there may come a day when you can do that no longer. Then there will be no *you* left to criticize the

mood or even enjoy it, but just the grumble itself going on forever like a machine.[94]

Many people today struggle with the idea of God's punishing disobedient people. When sin is seen as slavery, and hell—in one sense—as the freely chosen eternal slum of the universe, hell becomes much more comprehensible.

Here is an example of how I try to explain this: First, sin separates us from the presence of God (Isa. 59:2), which is the source of all joy (Ps. 16:11), love, wisdom, or good thing of any sort (James 1:17).

Second, to understand hell we must understand sin as slavery. Romans 1:21–25 tells us that we were built to live for God supremely, but instead we live for love, work, achievement, or morality to give us meaning and worth. Thus every person, religious or not, is worshiping something—idols, pseudo-saviors—to get their worth. But these things enslave us with guilt (if we fail to attain them), or anger (if someone blocks them from us), or fear (if they are threatened), or drivenness (since we must have them). Guilt, anger, fear, and drivenness are like fire that destroys us. Sin is worshiping anything but Jesus—and the wages of sin is slavery.

Perhaps the greatest paradox of all is that the people on Lewis's bus from hell are enslaved because they freely choose to be. They would rather have their freedom (as they define it) than salvation. Their tragic delusion is that if they glorified God, they would lose their human greatness (Gen. 3:4–5), but in reality their choice has ruined their human greatness. Hell is, as Lewis says, "the greatest monument to human freedom."[95]

---

94. C. S. Lewis, *The Great Divorce* (New York: HarperCollins, 2009), 77–78.

95. Timothy Keller, R. Albert Mohler Jr., J. I. Packer, and Robert Yarbrough, *Is Hell for Real or Does Everyone Go to Heaven?* (Grand Rapids: Zondervan, 2011), 77.

We are loved by a God
who has given us every
freedom we can imagine.

We are loved by a God who has given us every freedom we can imagine. He loves us enough to wait for us to love him in return. I can take my human freedom and choose my own master. So what will master me: drinking, addictive relationships, the love of money? Or will I make God my master, allowing his love to lead me away from a hellish existence here on earth and beyond, and toward a life of love and possibility?

FOR FURTHER THOUGHT

Can you think of some people or things in your life besides God that easily enslave and control you?

HOW CAN SOMEONE PURPOSELY CHOOSE TO GO TO HELL?

> Enter through the narrow gate. For wide is the gate and broad is the road that leads to destruction, and many enter through it. But small is the gate and narrow the road that leads to life, and only a few find it.
>
> **—MATTHEW 7:13-14**

During my years as a college softball coach, one of my most important jobs was helping athletes "own" the consequences of their decisions. One semester, Jessica asked my permission to join a campus club that met during our team's off-season workouts. I told Jessica that these decisions were hers. I also told her that there was another athlete competing for her position who might gain a physical advantage over her by attending the workouts. I told her that I would play the athlete who would best help our team win. The choice to join the club was hers and she should weigh the consequences of that choice.

In the same way, God gives each of us the freedom to make our choices and to live with the consequences that result. I don't think there is a Christian who better communicated this concept than Jonathan Edwards, a famous American preacher during the Great Awakening:

You are responsible for whether you go to hell. And here's why:

1. You gave no thought to your own salvation. You refused to take salvation seriously as God repeatedly commanded you to do. Why should God pay any attention to your pleas now? Should God care more about your happiness than you did for your own or for his glory? God cares about you because he loves you. But is he required to care for you now even when you did not care for yourself, or love yourself or respect his authority? You waited way too long to take care of your precious soul and you refused to make sacrifices for your own salvation. God called out to you! Neither obedience to God or the love of your own soul were enough to motivate you to make the simple changes required for your own eternal welfare. But now you expect God to be merciful and perform miracles on your behalf. You were urged to take care of your salvation before it was too late. You were told that the best time to do it was now and not wait until later, because if you waited too long and asked when it was too late, God would not hear you. But you didn't listen. You continued to do your own thing. Now you seek him in vain because God has rightly ordered that it is too late. You were told that you would regret it if you delayed, but again you did not listen. Now God has refused to show mercy and now you regret your decisions and want to repent. . . .

2. Not only have you neglected your salvation, you intentionally took steps that led to your undoing. You stubbornly continued to take pleasure in the sins that are now responsible for your damnation. Enough light was set before you to make the right

decisions, so you cannot plead ignorance. God told you that what you were doing was wrong and that it would lead to your destruction, but yet, you did it anyway. . . .

God is justified in leaving you in the mess you've created! You've stubbornly persisted on traveling the road to hell for a long time, despite God's counseling and commands. Time has passed and now you're nearing the end of your journey and getting closer to hell's gate. Use common sense and be aware of the dangerous situation you are in, the misery you are headed for. Don't blame God or call him unfair if he does not deliver you! You've intentionally destroyed yourself by going against God's repeated commands. . . . Now, how can you blame anyone but yourself if you are destroyed? Perhaps it was by his Spirit that he counseled you and warned you that opposing him will lead down the path to destruction. If God now decides to leave you there, whose fault is that? You wanted your own way and did not like it that God didn't agree with it. . . . Now that you're at the end of your journey, God has ceased to oppose you any further and agrees that you should have your own way, and he lets your soul be ruined. The path you chose to walk had a hand in this and the end result of misery was inevitable. . . . If God tries to restrain you from running into the fire, and you throw off the restraints of mercy and authority and continue to run stubbornly into the fire, you have no one to blame but yourself when you get burned.[96]

Like small children who choose not to listen to their parents' instructions, we adults can do the same thing in our relationship with God. We can use our free will to follow him or

---

96. Jonathan Edwards, "The Justice of God in the Damnation of Sinners" (Select Sermons) *Christian Classics Ethereal Library*. Text updated.

to go in the opposite direction. One path is narrow and leads to life, and the other path is wide and leads to destruction. The choice is always ours.

FOR FURTHER THOUGHT

Can you think of steps you have taken that lead toward a destructive path?

DO PEOPLE CHOOSE HELL OR SIN, AND WHAT IS THE DIFFERENCE?

Yet it was our weaknesses he carried;
    it was our sorrows that weighed him
        down. . . .
But he was pierced for our rebellion,
    crushed for our sins.
He was beaten so we could be whole.
    He was whipped so we could be
        healed.
All of us, like sheep, have strayed away.
    We have left God's paths to follow
        our own.
Yet the LORD laid on him
    the sins of us all.

—ISAIAH 53:4–6 NLT

HELL AS A CHOICE

I once heard a speaker tell an interesting story about imprisoned youth: when these teenagers were instructed to throw a tennis ball as hard as they could at the wall in front of them, not one of them stopped to think about what would happen next. Not one of them considered the possibility that a ball thrown directly in front of them would surely bounce back and hit them, slamming some of them in the face. These youth, like many adults, have not fully thought through the consequences of their actions.

Have the youth chosen to hit themselves in the face with a tennis ball or have they chosen to throw a tennis ball at the wall without considering the end result? Similarly, do people choose hell or do they choose sin? And what's the difference?

John Piper, a renowned Bible scholar, pastor, and author, wrote:

> What sinners want is not hell but sin. That hell is the inevitable consequence of unforgiven sin does not make the consequence desirable. It is not what people want—certainly not what they "most want." Wanting sin is no more equal to wanting hell than wanting chocolate is equal to wanting obesity. Or wanting cigarettes is equal to wanting cancer.
>
> Beneath this misleading emphasis on hell being what people "most want" is the notion that God does not "send" people to hell. But this is simply unbiblical. God certainly does send people to hell. He does pass sentence, and he executes it. Indeed, worse than that. God does not just "send," he "throws." "If anyone's name was not found written in the book of life, he was thrown (Greek *eblethe*) into the lake of fire" (Revelation 20:15; cf. Mark 9:47; Matthew 13:42; 25:30).

The reason the Bible speaks of people being "thrown" into hell is that no one will willingly go there, once they see what it really is. No one standing on the shore of the lake of fire jumps in. They do not *choose* it, and they will not *want* it. They have chosen sin. They have wanted sin. They do *not* want the punishment. When they come to the shore of this fiery lake, they must be thrown in.

When someone says that no one is in hell who doesn't want to be there, they give the false impression that hell is within the limits of what humans can tolerate. It inevitably gives the impression that hell is less horrible than Jesus says it is.

We should ask: *How did Jesus expect his audience to think and feel about the way he spoke of hell?* The words he chose were not chosen to soften the horror by being accommodating to cultural sensibilities. He spoke of a "fiery furnace" (Matthew 13:42), and "weeping and gnashing teeth" (Luke 13:28), and "outer darkness" (Matthew 25:30), and "their worm [that] does not die" (Mark 9:48), and "eternal punishment" (Matthew 25:46), and "unquenchable fire" (Mark 9:43), and being "cut in pieces" (Matthew 24:51).

These words are chosen to portray hell as an eternal, conscious experience that no one would or could ever "want" if they knew what they were choosing. Therefore, if someone is going to emphasize that people freely "choose" hell, or that no one is there who doesn't "want" to be there, surely he should make every effort to clarify that, when they get there, they will *not* want this.

Surely the pattern of Jesus—who used blazing words to blast the hell-bent blindness out of everyone—should be followed. Surely, we will grope for words that show no one, no one, *no one* will *want* to be in hell when they experience what it really is. Surely everyone who desires to save people from hell will not mainly stress that it is "wantable" or "choose-able," but that it is horrible beyond description—weeping, gnashing teeth, darkness, worm-eaten, fiery, furnace-like, dismembering, eternal, punishment, "an abhorrence to all flesh" (Isaiah 66:24).

I thank God, as a hell-deserving sinner, for Jesus Christ my Savior, who became a curse for me and suffered hellish pain that he might deliver me from the wrath to come. While there is time, he will do that for anyone who turns from sin and treasures him and his work above all.[97]

As Piper wrote, none of us want obesity or cancer; we want chocolate and cigarettes, right? God, more than anyone, understands why we do this. We want escape, relief, something to kill the pain and produce the joy we seek. We all ache and long for something this world cannot offer us. But there is a God in heaven who can offer us the very things we "most want." There is a God in heaven who is familiar with suffering and sorrow and wants to take those things from us. Will we let him?

FOR FURTHER THOUGHT

What are some quick and easy choices that you have made without first considering the consequences?

97. John Piper, "Desiring God," *Desiring God Foundation*, 2013, http://www.desiringgod.org/resource-library/taste-see-articles/ how-willingly-do-people-go-to-hell.

WHAT ARE SOME STORIES JESUS TOLD ABOUT HELL?

> With many similar parables Jesus spoke the word to them, as much as they could understand. He did not say anything to them without using a parable. But when he was alone with his own disciples, he explained everything.
>
> **—MARK 4:33–34**

Jesus spoke in parables or stories because he understood that stories are "smugglers of truth." How often have you found yourself identifying with a character in a book or movie, thinking, *I am just like that person*? Jesus used stories to illustrate truths about God and his coming kingdom. In the parable of the rich man and Lazarus, Jesus told a powerful story about how our lives on earth impact our futures in the next world or the world to come.

In the story, there is a poor man named Lazarus and a rich man who remains unnamed. (Perhaps the rich man is more like you and me than we would like to admit and that's why Jesus didn't give him a name?) Lazarus suffers through life while the rich man lives in comfort and ease. Day after day Lazarus presents the rich man with the opportunity to show mercy and compassion to him, but day after day, the rich man ignores Lazarus's suffering. How often do we ignore the suffering of others? How much do we live for ourselves and ignore the needs of others in the world around us?

The parable presents interesting ethical and moral dilemmas. How do we spend our days? How do we respond to the needs and suffering of others? What impact does our response have on our lives? In the parable, both men die and face their judgments.

As you read the parable, ask yourself: Whom do I identify with more: Lazarus or the rich man? What does this parable reveal about hell? And finally, how does God provide a way of escape? Listen to the words of Christ himself:

Jesus said, "There was a certain rich man who was splendidly clothed in purple and fine linen and who lived each day in luxury. At his gate lay a poor man named Lazarus who was covered with sores. As Lazarus lay there longing for scraps from the rich man's table, the dogs would come and lick his open sores.

"Finally, the poor man died and was carried by the angels to be with Abraham. The rich man also died and was buried, and his soul went to the place of the dead. There, in torment, he saw Abraham in the far distance with Lazarus at his side.

"The rich man shouted, 'Father Abraham, have some pity! Send Lazarus over here to dip the tip of his finger in water and cool my tongue. I am in anguish in these flames.'

"But Abraham said to him, 'Son, remember that during your lifetime you had everything you wanted, and Lazarus had nothing. So now he is here being comforted, and you are in anguish. And besides, there is a great chasm separating us.

> The choice for one's eternal
> destination seems to be
> made during one's time on
> earth, not after death.

No one can cross over to you from here, and no one can cross over to us from there.'

"Then the rich man said, 'Please, Father Abraham, at least send him to my father's home. For I have five brothers, and I want him to warn them so they don't end up in this place of torment.'

"But Abraham said, 'Moses and the prophets have warned them. Your brothers can read what they wrote.'

"The rich man replied, 'No, Father Abraham! But if someone is sent to them from the dead, then they will repent of their sins and turn to God.'

"But Abraham said, 'If they won't listen to Moses and the prophets, they won't listen even if someone rises from the dead.'"[98]

In this parable, Jesus described hell as a place of torment. A great chasm or separation exists between the heavenly realm and this place of torment so that no one can cross from one to the other. This speaks to the fixed nature of the afterlife. The choice for one's eternal destination seems to be made during one's time on earth, not after death.

FOR FURTHER THOUGHT

Which character do you relate to most in the story?

98. Luke 16:19–31 NLT.

HOW CAN I AVOID GOING TO HELL?

> For God so loved the world that he gave his one and only Son, that whoever believes in him shall not perish but have eternal life.
>
> **—JOHN 3:16**

It's important to start with the right question. Great questions can lead to greater understanding. Rather than ask, "How can I avoid going to hell?" it would be better to ask, "How can I choose heaven?" There's a classic country song called "Highway to Heaven" that mentions "walking up the King's highway" with lighter loads and joy in our hearts. So where is this highway and how can we choose it?

Two Christian teachers whom I respect a lot (Ken Boa and Robert Bowman) teamed up to write a book called *Sense and Nonsense about Heaven and Hell*. They said this:

> The New Testament is crystal clear in teaching that whoever will be saved, in any period of human history, will have been saved by the redemptive suffering, death, and resurrection of Jesus Christ. Two key statements in this regard, one from Jesus himself and one from the apostle Peter, are as explicit as they are famous:
>
> > I am the way, and the truth, and the life. No one comes to the Father except through me. (John 14:6)

And there is salvation in no one else, for there is no other name under heaven that has been given among people by which we must be saved. (Acts 4:12)

Why is it that people can only be saved if they are saved by Jesus?

(1) First of all, *they cannot save themselves*. People cannot make themselves good enough for God or make themselves right with God, based on what they do. This is the explicit teaching of Paul: "For 'no human being will be justified in his sight' by deeds prescribed by the law, for through the law comes the knowledge of sin" (Rom. 3:20). In other words, the Law of Moses does not give us a way to be justified, or considered right, in God's sight; instead, it simply tells us what sin is and shows that we are sinners.

If a person could get right with God by doing enough good works, then there might be some hope for people to gain eternal life without Christ's help. Unfortunately, none of us can pull it off, "for all have sinned and fall short of the glory of God, and they are now justified by his grace as a gift, through the redemption that is in Christ Jesus" (Rom. 3:23–24 ESV). This doesn't mean that Christians don't do good works—if they don't, their claim to believe is questionable—but that their relationship with God is not the result of their works but rather the result of God's gracious acceptance of them because of what Jesus did:

For by grace you have been saved through faith, and this is not your own doing; it is the gift of God—not the result of works, so that no one may boast. For we are what he has made us, created in Christ Jesus for good works, which God prepared beforehand to be our way of life. (Eph. 2:8–10)

If Christians cannot and do not save themselves by their works, it follows that no one else does either. Paul says explicitly that "no flesh" will be saved in that way.

(2) *God has chosen to save people throughout the world through his Son, Jesus Christ.* Those passages misunderstood by universal-ists as teaching that everyone will be saved come into play here. "For God so loved the world that he gave his only Son, so that everyone who believes in him may not perish but may have eternal life" (John 3:16). Jesus is the Savior for the world, dying to atone for the sins of people throughout the world, bringing reconciliation to the world and justification to all people (John 1:29; 4:42; 1 John 2:2; 4:14; Rom. 5:18; 2 Cor. 5:19; Col. 1:19–20; 1 Tim. 2:6). We can speculate all day long as to whether God might have chosen to save people in another way, but the fact is that we have no reliable way of knowing, and in fact Scripture says he has chosen this one way and no other.[99]

Perhaps the words of Christian author C. S. Lewis summarize it best:

> The Christian claim that Jesus is the only Savior is not a parochial, narrow-minded position. It is the truth.[100]

I choose to believe the Bible and the words of Jesus when he says that he is the way, the truth, and the life. There is no other way to get to heaven except through him. Following Jesus is the pathway, the "Highway to Heaven."

---

99. Kenneth D. Boa and Robert M. Bowman Jr., *Sense and Nonsense about Heaven and Hell* (Grand Rapids: Zondervan, 2007), 124.

100. Ibid.

FOR FURTHER THOUGHT

Do you believe that Jesus is the only way to be saved?

ONCE I DIE, AM I OUT OF CHANCES?

> Jesus answered, "I am the way and the truth and the life. No one comes to the Father except through me."
>
> **—JOHN 14:6**

"If only" is one of the most heart-wrenching phrases in the English language. Do you know why? Because it expresses regret, a human emotion sparked by insight or wisdom that came too late. Years ago, I lost a friend to suicide and the phrase "if only" haunted those of us who knew him for quite some time. I kept thinking, *If only I had said this . . .* or, *If only I had done that . . .*

Will people still have a chance to make a choice after death? Here is what Henry Edward Manning, a British Roman Catholic cardinal from the 1800s, said:

> At death, a judgment of the soul is passed and recorded before God. When we think of death, there is an awful sense that it's all over. Time has run out and it's been tied up, signed, sealed, and headed for eternity. Everything God had planned for us has been fulfilled. Life as we knew it is over and a new one has been assigned. The time for us to be inspired to live a life full of truth, grace and discipline to God's ways is now gone. All that was once possible has now come to fruition or

has become impossible. We have been put through the test and our time to be graded has now come. For better or for worse, our eternal state has now been fixed forever.

It's sad to realize that life as you'd known it is about to come to an end. You now know for certain you'll never be able to see your loved ones again. Or visit your favorite places or do your favorite things. Even the end of a hard life is met with sadness. The words, "no more," and "never again" are hard to hear let alone digest. We've experienced this when we've cried over loved ones that have died. However, if they belonged to Christ, there is no reason to be sad. But the realization that something has now completed its course, has come to a full end, and will now be gone forever, is heartbreaking. We don't understand it. It goes against all of our selfish desires. No more hope for a better future. No more chances to live a more devoted life. No more chances to fast more, worship more, or adore God more. No more encouraging words or comfort. No more warnings, discipline, corrections, or lessons to be learned. The patience of grace, the Church, and the loving rebukes of God have been tried and exhausted and brought to a full end. And it will be that way for eternity.

And when the end is near and we await our punishment, we'll not be able to stop ourselves from thinking, *"If only I'd known and paid more attention to the peace deep inside me. If only I'd stopped sinning when I still had the time. If only I'd listened when God tried to warn me, when people tried to let me know I needed to be more genuine, more respectful, and more*

We have been put through the test and our time to be graded has now come.

passionate about my relationship with Christ. But now, here I am and it's too late. I must now face eternity with these regrets. I go now with a memory full of sins and a heart threatening to burst through my chest from fear. My soul is dark from the choices I've made. Misery surrounds me. And now, because I am on my way to God, I don't have time to feel sorry for myself or to make any changes. My time has come and I am not fully prepared because I was weighed down by the thoughts of this world. God's presence and will buried beneath them. I now await my sentence. Will I hear the word, heaven? Or will I hear the word, hell!" For the confident, who say they have no fear of dying, surely, a great revelation such as this, will shake them to their core. They boast of no fear because they have no idea what death entails. It is God's fulfillment of our promise of salvation, or of our own sinful will. It is either the sealing of a saint, or the damnation of a reprobate soul.[101]

I can't erase the words "if only" from our vocabulary, so I try to speak up when I should and to keep the important things first. I don't want to get to the end of my life here on earth and say, "If only I had loved more" or, "If only I had trusted God more." Do you? Let's make the most of the days we've been given and make wise decisions here and now. Don't wait.

FOR FURTHER THOUGHT

Do you need to make a decision today about whether you believe that Jesus is the way, the truth, and the life and that no one comes to the Father except through him?

---

101. Henry Edward Manning, "Sermon 19: The Tearfulness of Death" (Sermons. Volume Third) *Christian Classics Ethereal Library*. Text updated.

The Limbourg Brothers;
Tundal's Hell, from *Tres Riches Heures*;
c. 1416

"Once I was free in the shackles of sin:
Free to be tempted, just bound to give in;
Free to be captive to any desire;
Free to eternally burn in hell's fire.
'Til Someone bought me and called me His slave:
Bound by commands I am free to obey;
Captive by beauty I'm free to adore —
Sentenced to sit at His feet evermore."

—John MacArthur

"He supposed that even in Hell, people got an occasional sip of water, if only so they could appreciate the full horror of unrequited thirst when it set in again."

—Stephen King, *Full Dark, No Stars*

"This is the deepest level of hell, where the fallen angel Satan himself resides. His wings flap eternally, producing chilling cold winds that freeze the thick ice found in Cocytus. The three faces of Satan, black, red, and yellow, can be seen with mouths gushing bloody foam and eyes forever weeping, as they chew on the three traitors, Judas, Brutus, and Cassius. This place is furthest removed from the source of all light and warmth. Sinners here are frozen deep in the ice, faces out, eyes and mouths frozen shut. Traitors against God,

country, family, and benefactors lament
their sins in this frigid pit of despair."

    —Dante's *Inferno*

"The Son of Man will send out his angels,
and they will weed out of his kingdom
everything that causes sin and all who
do evil. They will throw them into the
blazing furnace, where there will be
weeping and gnashing of teeth."

    —Jesus (Matt. 13:41–42)

"There shall be weeping, an expression
of great sorrow and anguish; not a gush
of tears, which gives present ease, but
constant weeping, which is constant
torment; and the gnashing of teeth is
an expression of the greatest rage and
indignation."

    —Matthew Henry

And the devil, who deceived them, was thrown into the lake of burning sulfur, where the beast and the false prophet had been thrown. They will be tormented day and night for ever and ever.

Then I saw a great white throne and him who was seated on it. The earth and the heavens fled from his presence, and there was no place for them. And I saw the dead, great and small, standing before the throne, and books were opened.

Another book was opened, which is the book of life. The dead were judged according to what they had done as recorded in the books. The sea gave up the dead that were in it, and death and Hades gave up the dead that were in them, and each person was judged according to what they had done. Then death and Hades were thrown into the lake of fire. The lake of fire is the second death. Anyone whose name was not found written in the book of life was thrown into the lake of fire.

—REVELATION 20:10–15

HOW BAD IS HELL, REALLY?

I am the Living One; I was dead, and now look, I am alive for ever and ever! And I hold the keys of death and Hades.

—REVELATION 1:18

Years ago I heard about one of the worst child-abuse cases in California's history. In *A Child Called "It"* Dave Pelzer recounted how his alcoholic mother would chain him in the garage like a dog and make him eat dog food, how she'd beat him and say cruel things to him. This abuse went on for years. The horrors recounted in this book tell of the cruelty humans can have toward each other. Is this what hell will be like? Punishment and sadistic torture? How bad is hell, really? R. C. Sproul, pastor and author of the series *Heaven*, explains:

Almost all the biblical teaching about hell comes from the lips of Jesus.

We have often heard statements such as "War is hell" or "I went through hell." These expressions are, of course, not taken literally. Rather, they reflect our tendency to use the word *hell* as a descriptive term for the most ghastly human experience possible. Yet no human experience in this world is actually comparable to hell. If we try to imagine the worst of all possible suffering in the here and now we have not yet stretched our imaginations to reach the dreadful reality of hell.

Hell is trivialized when it is used as a common curse word. To use the word lightly may be a halfhearted human attempt to take the concept lightly or to treat it in an amusing way. We tend to joke about things most frightening to us in a futile effort to declaw and defang them, reducing their threatening power.

There is no biblical concept more grim or terror-invoking than the idea of hell. It is so unpopular with us that few would give credence to it at all except that it comes to us from the teaching of Christ Himself.

Almost all the biblical teaching about hell comes from the lips of Jesus. It is this doctrine, perhaps more than any other, that strains even the Christian's loyalty to the teaching of Christ. Modern Christians have pushed the limits of minimizing hell in an effort to sidestep or soften Jesus' own teaching. The Bible describes hell as a place of outer darkness, a lake of fire, a place of weeping and gnashing of teeth, a place of eternal separation from the blessings of God, a prison, a place of torment where the worm doesn't turn or die. These graphic images of eternal punishment provoke the question, should we take these descriptions literally or are they merely symbols?

I suspect they are symbols, but I find no relief in that. We must not think of them as being merely symbols. It is probable that the sinner in hell would prefer a literal lake of fire as his eternal abode to the reality of hell represented in the lake of fire image. If these images are indeed symbols, then we must conclude that the reality is worse than the symbol suggests. The function of symbols is to point beyond themselves to a higher or more intense state of actuality than the symbol itself can contain. That Jesus used the most awful symbols imaginable to describe hell is no comfort to those who see them simply as symbols.

A breath of relief is usually heard when someone declares, "Hell is a symbol for separation from God." To be separated from God for eternity is no great threat to the impenitent person. The ungodly want nothing more than to be separated from God. Their problem in hell will not be separation from God, it will be the presence of God that will torment them. In hell, God will be present in the fullness of His divine wrath. He will be there to exercise His just punishment of the damned. They will know Him as an all-consuming fire.

No matter how we analyze the concept of hell it often sounds to us as a place of cruel and unusual punishment. If, however, we can take any comfort in the concept of hell, we can take it in the full assurance that there will be no cruelty there. It is impossible for God to be cruel. Cruelty involves inflicting a punishment that is more severe or harsh than the crime. Cruelty in this sense is unjust. God is incapable of inflicting an unjust punishment. The Judge of all the earth

What the Bible Says About Hell

Overwhelming Destruction
2 Samuel 22:5-6

Absence of God's Presence
2 Thessalonians 1:9

A Bottomless Pit
Revelation 9:2

**Worms That Don't Die
and Eat Dead Bodies**
Isaiah 66:24

A Place of Torment
Luke 16:23

Lake of Fire
Revelation 20:15

**A Place of
Sorrows**
Matthew 13:49-50

**A Place of
No Rest**
Revelation 14:11

**Gates of
Death/Hades**
Job 17:16

**Fiery Lake of
Burning Sulfur**
Revelation 19:20

**A Place of Outer
Darkness**
Matthew 22:13

Chains of Darkness
2 Peter 2:4, 9

Blazing Furnace
Matthew 13:41-42

An Unquenchable Fire
Matthew 3:12

© *TheBiblePeople.com*

will surely do what is right. No innocent person will ever suffer at His hand.

Perhaps the most frightening aspect of hell is its eternality. People can endure the greatest agony if they know it will ultimately stop. In hell there is no such hope. The Bible clearly teaches that the punishment is eternal. The same word is used for both eternal life and eternal death. Punishment implies pain. Mere annihilation, which some have lobbied for, involves no pain. Jonathan Edwards, in preaching on Revelation 6:15–16 said, "Wicked men will hereafter earnestly wish to be turned to nothing and forever cease to be that they may escape the wrath of God." (John H. Gerstner, *Jonathan Edwards on Heaven and Hell* [Orlando: Ligonier Ministries, 1991], 75.)

Hell, then, is an eternity before the righteous, everburning wrath of God, a suffering torment from which there is no escape and no relief. Understanding this is crucial to our drive to appreciate the work of Christ and to preach His gospel.[102]

Unfortunately, as humans living in a broken world, we are familiar with pain and suffering. Many of us have walked through lives affected by poverty, violent crime, mental illness, and more. We have had glimpses into the reality of hell. As we think about this reality, may we remember that Jesus made his descent into hell after which he ascended into heaven and now sits at the right hand of the Father. It is through faith in him that we are set free from the reality of hell.

---

102. R. C. Sproul, *Essential Truths of the Christian Faith* (Wheaton, IL: Tyndale House, 1992), 285–287.

FOR FURTHER THOUGHT

Are there certain beliefs in Christianity that are preventing you from trusting and hoping in Jesus?

WHAT DOES JESUS SAY ABOUT HELL?

> Do not be afraid of those who kill the body but cannot kill the soul. Rather, be afraid of the One who can destroy both soul and body in hell.
>
> **—MATTHEW 10:28**

"I imagine hell like this: Italian punctuality, German humour and English wine," quipped Peter Ustinov, a British actor and writer. All kidding aside, what will hell really be like? And to whom should we pose such important questions? Actors? Authors? Pastors? It seems that we can learn a lot from the writings and teachings of others, but why not pose the question to Jesus himself? What did he have to say about hell? Quite a lot, actually.

Robert Yarbrough recounted Jesus' words this way:

Jesus gives a central place to hell in his best-known recorded sermon (Matt. 5–7). He warns against hateful anger, because "anyone who says, 'You fool!' will be in danger of the fire of hell" (5:22). He warns against adulterous looks and actions, lecherous sins of the eye and hand. Gouge out the eye, cut off the hand, Jesus says, because "it is better for you to lose one part of your body than for your whole body to be thrown into hell" (5:29–30). Although it is widely agreed that he overstates here for rhetorical effect, even as a figure of speech his words are graphic.

Later in his ministry Jesus repeats these statements in a different connection (18:9), and he makes it clear that hell involves a fire that never ends: "It is better for you to enter life maimed or crippled than to have two hands or two feet and be thrown into eternal fire" (18:8). He makes it clear that people face vastly different eternal destinies: "Enter through the narrow gate. For wide is the gate and broad is the road that leads to destruction, and many enter through it. But small is the gate and narrow the road that leads to life, and only a few find it" (7:13–14).

Such passages suggest that Jesus viewed hell as real, awful, and "eternal" (we will discuss the meaning of this word more fully below). Jesus also used the fear of hell as a motivator, inciting people to take painful measures now, if necessary, to avoid a fate worse than mere physical death later.

When Jesus sent out the Twelve, he realized they would be harassed, hated, and persecuted. The temptation to cowardice or compromise would be strong. Jesus' own example of courage under fire was one incentive for them to take to heart: "A student is not above the teacher, nor a servant above his master. . . . If the head of the house has been called Beelzebul, how much more the members of his household!" (Matt. 10:24–25). Yet Jesus gave them

When Jesus sent out the Twelve, he realized they would be harassed, hated, and persecuted.

another incentive as well: the fear of God, whose disapproval is more terrible than any harm inflicted by people. In this connection Christ states: "Do not be afraid of those who kill the body but cannot kill the soul. Rather, be afraid of the One who can destroy both soul and body in hell" (10:28).

Once again we see Christ appeal to hell, this time as a positive motivator to grasp the nettle of Christian service boldly even when it involves loss, pain, and earthly destruction. Temporary discomfort here and now is preferable to permanent calamity in the age to come.

The passages above were addressed to his disciples. But Jesus extends this grim prospect to those who oppose his message, including the religious leaders of Jerusalem and Judea. He calls these leaders "hypocrites," in part because by opposing him they "shut the door of the kingdom of heaven in people's faces" (Matt. 23:13). Jesus accused them of turning people away from his message, producing a convert who is then "twice as much a child of hell" as they themselves (23:15). In biblical usage the term "child/son of" usually means physical descendent. But it also has a metaphorical meaning. "A child of hell" is someone whose life shows the same qualities as the religious leaders. Here Jesus' teaching implies that hell exerts influence on people to remain in their natural, unsaved moral condition rather than responding with a whole heart to Jesus' call to repentance and personal trust in him. Hell is thus a sphere of influence in the present world as well as a destination in the world to come.[103]

Jesus had a lot to say about hell. In fact, it was one of the topics he frequently talked about when teaching his followers or large crowds of people. It helps me to remember that Jesus

---

103. Timothy Keller, R. Albert Mohler Jr., J. I. Packer, and Robert Yarbrough, *Is Hell for Real or Does Everyone Go to Heaven?* (Grand Rapids: Zondervan, 2011), 26.

taught about hell in order to warn people and to turn them back to the heart of a loving Father.

FOR FURTHER THOUGHT

To whom do you listen as an authority on the subject of hell?

WHAT DO WE LOSE IN HELL?

> And if your eye causes you to stumble, pluck it out. It is better for you to enter the kingdom of God with one eye than to have two eyes and be thrown into hell.
>
> —MARK 9:47

My wife and I took our son to San Diego's Sea World when he was three years old. We sat in the splash zone at Shamu's show and got ourselves thoroughly soaked on a hot day. As we walked out of the show, we found ourselves trying to push through the crowd while wringing out our clothes, laughing at the new memories, and enjoying the good time. A few moments passed before my wife and I realized that our tiny son was missing. Had he slipped through the crowd? Did someone take him? Did he find a way back to the whale tank? I'll never forget the sheer panic I felt and how quickly my mind raced to the most awful, darkest possibilities. My heart was pounding and aching all at the same time. A few minutes later, we spotted him when a kind, tall gentleman hoisted him on his shoulders so we could find each other in the crowd.

When I think of the potential pain of being cut off from a family member, I wonder how minimal that must be when compared to the pain of being cut off from God himself. What would life be like if the connection with God—and all things good—was severed? That, indeed, would be hell.

John Wesley, one of the most famous preachers in Christian history, said this:

> *Paena Damni*, which means "the punishment of loss," is what happens immediately when a person's unsaved soul is separated from the body. In an instant, that person's soul loses every pleasure ever known to man. They are no longer able to see, smell, taste, hear, or touch. The bodily organs that were once so essential to their physical health have now rotted. Everything that once brought a smile to their face has now been eternally removed.
>
> Those things are forgotten in the dark regions of hell. But if by chance they are remembered, they will only be remembered with pain, knowing that those pleasures are now gone forever. The imagination of the lost soul has also come to an end. Never again will they be able to escape into the comforting recesses of the mind, as there are no such privileges in the tombs of hell. There is nothing beautiful in the dark. Especially when the only light will

These lost souls have been separated from everything they once loved in this world.

be the light that will emanate from angry flames. There will be nothing new to look forward to, the only scenery being one of endless agonizing torment. The groans and shrieks of the tortured will be their music. Weeping, wailing, and gnashing of teeth will surround them. Curses and blasphemies against God will taunt them. There is no honor among the lost souls in the bottomless pit. They are now considered the sons and daughters of shame and everlasting contempt.

These lost souls have been separated from everything they once loved in this world. And it's not over, because at that very same instant they will also endure another loss. The loss of all of the people that they once loved. These unsaved souls have been ripped away from their wives, husbands, parents, and children. And some from the one friend that knew them like none other. But the joy they once shared with these loved ones has now vanished. There are no relationships in hell. No friendships.

They will also sense a greater loss. A loss more devastating than anything else they lost while they were alive in this world. They have lost their place in Abraham's bosom, their chance to dwell with God in paradise. No one on earth has yet been able to fully know the joy saved souls will experience in the garden of God. In this society of angels, saved souls will also be in the presence of some of the wisest men that have lived from the beginning of time. And they too, will be blessed with increased knowledge. And only then will they be able to fully understand the value of the sacrifices they have made.

But as happy as these saved souls are that they are in paradise, they will be even happier when they realize they are also being prepared for something far greater. Paradise is only the porch of heaven, and heaven is where the spirits of men and women are made perfect. Only in heaven is there fullness of joy, where they will experience the pleasures that are at God's right hand forevermore. The unsaved and tortured souls in hell will feel this loss and it will be added to the completion of their misery. They will be able to feel and fully understand once and for all that God is the center of everything and that a spirit made for God will have no rest outside of His presence.[104]

All that can be lost is lost in hell. There are no friendships and no relationships. There is no love or joy or anything that will make you smile. Doesn't that sound horrible? In Jesus, though, we know that what was once lost, is now found. He is the one who pursues the lost, embraces lost souls, and heals broken hearts.

FOR FURTHER THOUGHT
Who is the one person you could not stand to lose?

---

104. John Wesley, (Text on hell from the 1872 edition) "Sermons on Several Occasions," *Christian Classics Ethereal Library.* Text updated.

HOW CAN I BE HAPPY IN HEAVEN WHEN I KNOW PEOPLE IN HELL?

> He will wipe every tear from their eyes. There will be no more death or mourning or crying or pain, for the old order of things has passed away.
>
> **—REVELATION 21:4**

How can I be happy if someone I love is in hell? Honestly, I don't know, but it reminds me of my childhood summers spent exploring Disneyland, the "happiest place on earth." While riding Peter Pan, eating cherry sour balls, and watching the electric light parade, I was in "heaven." I had nothing to cry or complain about. My mind was fully occupied with goodness.

C. S. Lewis's thoughts on the topic as revealed in his work *The Great Divorce* are some of the most profound. Here is a look at his book by literary scholar Wayne Martindale:

> Lewis's best answer to the objection that no one could be perfectly or justly happy in Heaven knowing some were in Hell, especially if our loved ones are among them, appears in *The Great Divorce*. The scene at issue involves a woman named Sarah Smith and her husband, Frank. Sarah, now glorious in her resurrection body, comes from Heaven to its threshold to meet Frank, who has come up from Hell. The wise guide, MacDonald, explains to the watching narrator that "already there is joy enough in the little finger of a great saint such as yonder lady to waken all the dead things of the universe into

life."[105] She is Sarah Smith from Golders Green, which is like saying Jane Doe from the slums, a "nobody" by the world's standards, but a "saint" by Heaven's, and in appearance, a goddess to the narrator.

Next, the narrator sees a figure looking like a "Tragedian" in a bad play, holding a string as though he had an "organ-grinder's" monkey on the end. The monkey turns out to be Frank, and the Tragedian a projection of his besetting sin, pity. By pity Frank manipulated everyone around him in his earthly life, striking the pose of a man injured or about to be injured by another's words or acts. The Tragedian is large and Frank a small ghost because there is more sinful pity than human soul by now. Though Sarah addresses Frank directly, he is so fully controlled by his sin that the Tragedian does his speaking for him. Frank has come to the edge of Heaven only to enjoy the self-gratifying feeling of having been missed and to see Sarah's misery at her loneliness. He discovers that there are no needs in Heaven and that Sarah has now learned what love really is because she is "in Love Himself," that is, in Christ.

When she says her love for him on earth was mostly the need to be loved, though having some of the real thing, she only says what is true of all of us, but for Frank it is another opportunity to wallow in his hurt feelings. He announces that he had rather see her dead at his feet than to hear he is not needed. All the while "merriment danced in her eyes," and joy poured from her countenance. To Frank's surprise and dismay, she is cheerful throughout the conversation in which she attempts to persuade him to give up his manipulating ways long enough to think of something besides himself and thereby move toward Heaven. She speaks of the

105. C. S. Lewis, *The Great Divorce* (New York: HarperCollins, 2009), 120.

joy she has entered and exudes, and issues an invitation for him to join her. Frank prefers the misery of his pet sin to abandoning it for the fullness of joy. In the end, the Ghost disappears, and only the Tragedian sulks back to Hell; he becomes the sin he has chosen.

To the narrator's surprise, Sarah goes rejoicing on her way, singing a psalm of praise to God, who "fills her brim full with immensity of life" and "leads her to see the world's desire."[106] The narrator, as usual, asks his guide the question that brews in our own minds: How is it possible that she could be happy when her husband languishes forever in Hell? MacDonald, giving always Lewis's view, distinguishes the "action of Pity," which is ever ready to sacrifice for another's good and is eternal, and the "passion of pity," which is used as a weapon to blackmail others for supposed personal gain . . . This weapon, used by the evil against the good, "will be broken."[107] Hell will not be allowed to blackmail Heaven. . . . The logic and justice of Lewis's position hinges on choice. God will not force someone to choose Heaven. In other words, he will not force someone to love him because love must be given. It always involves surrender.[108]

In the end, good triumphs over evil, not the other way around. God's presence will eclipse all sorrow. Death will be swallowed up in victory. Our minds and emotions will be made new! Laughter and bliss will be ours. Like beloved children in a place of pure joy and safety, we won't have room for worry

---

106. Ibid., 134. The psalm is reminiscent of Psalm 91.

107. Ibid., 136. Much of the paragraph is a paraphrase of this page.

108. Taken from *Beyond the Shadowlands: C.S. Lewis on Heaven and Hell* by Wayne Martindale, © 2005, pp. 147–149. Used by permission of Crossway, a publishing ministry of Good News Publishers, Wheaton, IL 60187, www.crossway.org.

> In the end, good triumphs over evil, not the other way around.

or sadness. Perfect trust and peace in God's goodness will finally be ours.

FOR FURTHER THOUGHT

How might your concern for someone's eternal salvation motivate you to act today?

Dieric Bouts;
Descent into Hell (detail);
c. 1468

HELL AND THE FINAL JUDGMENT

"Heaven might shine bright, but so do flames."

—Neal Shusterman, *Everwild*

"I deserved hell; Jesus took my hell; there is nothing left for me but His heaven."

—Donald Grey Barnhouse

"Christianity teaches that this life is not the only life, and there is a final judgment in which all earthly accounts are settled."

—Dinesh D'Souza

"The day of judgment will be a day when the skeletons come out of the closets! And each of us will be standing there to face the record."

—Adrian Rogers

"Those whimpering Stateside young people will wake up on the Day of Judgment condemned to worse fates than these demon-fearing Indians, because, having a Bible, they were bored with it— while these never heard of such a thing as writing."

—Jim Elliot

"He who loveth God with all his heart feareth not death, nor punishment, nor judgment, nor hell, because perfect love giveth sure access to God. But he who still delighteth in sin, no marvel if he is afraid of death and judgment."

—Thomas à Kempis

When the Son of Man comes in his glory, and all the angels with him, he will sit on his glorious throne. All the nations will be gathered before him, and he will separate the people one from another as a shepherd separates the sheep from the goats. He will put the sheep on his right and the goats on his left.

Then the King will say to those on his right, "Come, you who are blessed by my Father; take your inheritance, the kingdom prepared for you since the creation of the world. . . ."

Then he will say to those on his left, "Depart from me, you who are cursed, into the eternal fire prepared for the devil and his angels."

—MATTHEW 25:31–34, 41

HOW IS ETERNITY IN HELL A FAIR PUNISHMENT FOR SIN?

Whoever sows to please their flesh, from the flesh will reap destruction.
—GALATIANS 6:8

I remember a time in middle school when my math teacher kicked me out of class for pointing out a mistake she had made on the board. I didn't think I had been disrespectful, but I must have been. I remember sitting on the hallway floor, crying over the injustice of being tossed from class for being right. From my perspective, the penalty seemed wildly out of proportion.

Sometimes we look at hell and the consequences of our sin the same way. We look at a friend who is generally a good person but occasionally drives too fast, tells a few white lies, or pays their housekeeper under the table. While all those may be sins, are they worthy of the same punishment as a Charles Manson? That's the wrong perspective. Hell is not a consequence for a specific sin or the list of sins we may commit over a lifetime. It is the eternal punishment and inevitable destination for those who have rejected God and his plan for salvation. This completely holy God cannot be in the presence of sin of any kind—no matter how small it seems.

Ken Boa, a powerful writer and Bible teacher, wrote the following:

The purpose of Hell is not to make those who go there better people or to help them see the error of their ways and come to repentance. Hell is not like the Betty Ford Clinic. It is not even like a modern prison, where most prisoners are encouraged to become rehabilitated so that they may reenter society as useful citizens. The purpose of Hell is to punish sinners. It is about retribution, not restoration.

The evidence for this thesis in the New Testament is beyond reasonable challenge. God's final disposition toward the wicked is consistently described throughout the New Testament as one of anger and wrath (Matt. 3:7; 18:34; Luke 3:7; John 3:36; Rom. 2:5, 8–9; 5:9; 9:22; Eph. 2:3; 5:6; Col. 3:6; 1 Thess. 1:10; 5:9; Rev. 6:16–17; 14:10; 19:15). Jesus compares Hell to a prison where offenders are tortured for their crimes (Matt. 5:25–26; 18:34–35; Luke 12:47–48, 58–59). Those in Hell will receive "eternal punishment" (Matt. 25:46) . . . being cast into the eternal fire prepared for the Devil and his angels (Matt. 25:41). Peter said that "the unrighteous," like wicked angels, are being kept "under punishment" while awaiting the final judgment (2 Pet. 2:9). . . .

Moreover, Paul writes to Christians in Thessalonica that Christ will "repay with affliction those who afflict you," and that when he comes, he will be "inflicting vengeance" (2 Thess. 1:6–9). *Ekdikesis* can also be translated "revenge" or "retribution"; Jesus is going to make them pay! That may sound shocking to some people today, but not to those who have suffered greatly for their faith in Christ. . . .

Hell is not like
the Betty Ford Clinic.

Some might suppose that Jesus' comparisons of the wicked being punished in Hell to prisoners suffering until they "pay" their debt (Matt. 5:25–26; 18:34–35; Luke 12:58–59) might offer such hope. Not so. In Jesus' parable of the unforgiving servant, his debt to the master (representing God) is said to be ten thousand talents, whereas his fellow servant's debt to him was a hundred denarii (Matt. 18:24, 28). . . .

Jesus' parable directly challenges the common sentiment that sending someone to Hell for eternity is out of proportion, that the punishment does not fit the crime. He characterizes the "debt" that we owe to God as an astronomical sum. The servant's debt to his master is *a million times greater* than the substantial debt his fellow servant owed to him. That is the way Jesus pictures for us the enormity of our sin in God's eyes.

Lest Jesus' teaching on Hell be misunderstood, it is essential to the doctrine that whatever punishment is meted out in Hell will be just. Critics sometimes caricature Christianity as teaching that a kindly old nonreligious grandmother will get the same punishment as Adolf Hitler. This is simply not the case. God is not sadistic or in any way unjust. His anger or wrath is a righteous anger. Whatever Hell will be like and whoever ends up there, it will not be unfair, unjust, or out of proportion.[109]

When I think about the justice and punishment found in hell, I admit that I feel overwhelmed. While I can't fully understand it, I know that God is just and good, and that he has designed hell as the appropriate place for those who reject

---

109. Kenneth D. Boa and Robert M. Bowman Jr., *Sense and Nonsense about Heaven and Hell* (Grand Rapids: Zondervan, 2007), 102–104.

him. But I also know that God doesn't want anyone to face eternal death or to suffer forever in hell. That's why he provided a way toward new life through faith in his Son, Jesus. Whenever I think about the justice and judgment of hell, I find myself remembering the cross too.

FOR FURTHER THOUGHT

In what way does the reality of hell help you appreciate the power of the cross?

HOW CAN A **LOVING** GOD **SEND** PEOPLE TO **HELL**?

> Far be it from you to do such a thing—to kill the righteous with the wicked, treating the righteous and the wicked alike. Far be it from you! Will not the Judge of all the earth do right?
>
> **—GENESIS 18:25**

Growing up, I had a friend whose grandmother would reprimand us when we got in trouble: "You've made your bed, now lie in it." What she meant was, "You've done this to yourself, so now you have to suffer the consequences." I wonder: If God has given every man and woman free will or the freedom to choose, then is he sending people to hell or are they sending themselves? Isn't it my choices that lead me down the road that leads to heaven or hell? Have we made our beds, but then blame God for making us lie down in them?

Francis Chan teamed up with author and teacher Preston Sprinkle to write *Erasing Hell*. Here's how they answer this question:

> Can God be loving and still send people to hell? . . . We must answer yes. Here are three reasons why:
>
> First, God is love, but He also *defines* what love is. We don't have the license to define love according to our own standards and sensibilities. We often assume that love means achieving the ultimate happiness of everyone you are able to. If this were love, then yes, hell would be incompatible with God's love. But Scripture doesn't define God's love in this way. Love is part of who God is. And God defines what love is. God does not *have* to save everyone for Him to *show love*. Love, in other words, is essentially wrapped up in the character of God. Though God acts in ways that *seem* unloving by our standards, they are not unloving by His standards— and His standards are the ones that matter.
>
> Second, we must understand the love of God in light of His other characteristics. God is love, but He is also holy and just, and He frequently pours out wrath toward sin. In fact, God sometimes withholds certain attributes in order to exercise others. For instance, God withholds His wrath to exercise mercy. God withholds justice to pour out His grace. Of course, God *could* choose to lavish all humanity with His mercy and therefore choose to withhold His wrath toward everyone. But the Bible doesn't support this.
>
> Third, and to my mind most importantly, we must understand God's love in light of God's freedom. As we have seen in this book, God, as the Creator, is free to do

whatever He sees best. He is compelled by none other than Himself. And God's freedom means—though it's difficult to swallow—that God *can* withhold love (Rom. 9). It's a logical (and theological) mistake to think that God can't be loving unless He saves everyone. Such an assumption, while seeking to cherish the love of God, violates His freedom and sovereignty.

I'm not at all trying to minimize the pain we feel when we think about the unsaved being tormented in hell, nor am I suggesting that we simply snuff our emotions and move on with our lives: Remember Paul's anguish (Rom. 9:2–3). All I'm suggesting is that as the all-powerful, all-wise Creator of the universe, God does what is just, right, and loving in a much more profound way than we can possibly imagine. We must cling to Abraham's words in Genesis 18:25: "Shall not the Judge of all the earth do what is just?"[110]

In the same way that I have the human freedom to choose, God has freedom to choose. It is both my struggle and burden simply to trust that God—the Judge of all the earth—will do what is just, good, and loving, much like my friend's wise grandma who made us suffer the consequences of our poor choices when I was a young boy.

FOR FURTHER THOUGHT

Are your life choices leading you down the path toward death or life?

---

110. Francis Chan and Preston Sprinkle, *Erasing Hell: What God Said About Eternity, and the Things We've Made Up* (Colorado Springs, CO: David C. Cook, 2011), 162–164.

WHY IS JUDGMENT DAY GOOD NEWS?

> Righteousness and justice are the foundation of his throne.
> —PSALM 97:2

Be open-minded. Don't judge. Accept everyone. Most of us in American culture grew up being taught, "Don't judge people. Don't be so closed-minded." As the Beatles sang, you've got to "live and let live," right? So if judgment is such a bad thing, why would God put us through it? What exactly is Judgment Day?

Trevin Wax, the author of *Counterfeit Gospels: Rediscovering the Good News in a World of False Hope*, explained:

> I don't know what you think of when you hear the phrase "Judgment Day," but it sounds dreadful to me. My mind races to end-of-the-world movies that describe an apocalypse of epic proportions. And even when I remember that I need to let the Bible—not Hollywood—shape my understanding of judgment, I find many reasons to be terrified. Just think: *God's holy and righteous judgment being poured out on all that is wrong with us and the world.* Yikes!
>
> But there is something comforting about God's judgment, something that the writers of the Catechism recognize as integral to the gospel story. It's something we don't want to miss. . . .
>
> Humans are united by a desire for justice. We realize that life isn't fair. And yet for some reason, we also think it *should* be fair. The Bible teaches that life isn't fair *now,* and yet Scripture still points to a day when wrongs will be righted

and justice will be served. God will straighten things out once and for all.

That's why the idea of Christ's return in judgment brings comfort. To those who suffer at the hands of the unjust, it is comforting to hold on to the promise that one day all will be made right. This upside-down, crazy world will not go on in its current state forever. God will execute justice. The righteousness of God will be evident for all to see, and the knowledge of the Lord will flood the earth as the waters cover the sea.

But there is also a scary side to the idea of a world of perfect justice. Just think: If God were to return and purge the world of evil, what would happen to us? Would we be able to inhabit a perfect world? What happens when we realize that we are part of the problem, not just the ones longing for a solution?

When we take our place within the cosmic story of redemption, we come to realize that we are more than passive victims of evil's consequences. We are evil insurrectionists, rebels against the good and loving authority of God our Creator. . . . We thirst for justice, but once we consider the fairness of God, we quickly discover that Christ's return can only be good news if we have found mercy in God's sight. . . .

Once we understand God's judgment as putting an end to all that is wrong with the world (war, famine, disease, etc.), then we can understand why even the apostle Paul viewed judgment as part of his gospel. . . .

God is not a bipolar deity—one side wrathful and angry, the other loving and merciful.

This upside-down, crazy world will not go on in its current state forever.

Love is his essential attribute, but this love is not like the sentimental love we think of today. God's love is holy. It is jealous. The wrath of God is based in His love. The idea of biblical judgment not only assures us of future justice. It also gives us a clearer picture of the love of God. . . .

God hates sin because of what it does to us. He hates sin because of what it does to His good creation. He rages against sin because of His great love for His children. But it's not enough to say that God will judge sin and restore creation *for our benefit*. This is a step in the right direction, but it leaves out a crucial component of sin and judgment. God is wrathful toward sin—not only because of what it does to us, but also because of what it does to *Him*. It dishonors His name. . . .

God the Judge has promised to completely wipe out the evil of the world. And yet, He loves us. In His grace, He is the righteous judge and the gracious redeemer. His wrath toward evil is poured out upon His only Son on the cross. Justice and mercy are not at war with one another. They meet at the cross. And we can find both judgment and mercy as good news. We need only recognize our guilt in light of God's holiness and then bask in forgiveness in light of God's grace.[111]

Judgment Day for those who are in Christ is not to be feared, but to be looked forward to with hopeful expectation. We know that God, the just and holy judge, will make decisions with perfect wisdom and mercy. And so we can look forward to the day when he rights every wrong and heals every hurt.

---

111. Trevin Wax, *Counterfeit Gospels: Rediscovering the Good News in a World of False Hope* (Chicago: Moody Publishers, 2011), 80–82. Used with permission.

FOR FURTHER THOUGHT

Why does the idea of God's judgment make you anxious or uncomfortable?

WHAT IS **JUDGMENT** DAY **FOR UNBELIEVERS?**

> But only a fearful expectation of judgment and of raging fire that will consume the enemies of God.
>
> **—HEBREWS 10:27**

When I received my notice for jury duty, I was completely confident that I could be an impartial judge. However, when I heard the charges against the defendant during jury selection I became the exact opposite: judgmental and biased! As I continued to listen to the circumstances of the crime, it became pretty clear that I would not be able to be a fair juror. I wasn't at all surprised when I was not selected to serve on the jury.

How do you decide a person's guilt or innocence? When I think about the Day of Judgment, I can't imagine standing before God, a holy judge, without a defense attorney. As a believer my defense attorney is Jesus. But what about nonbelievers? How will they face judgment without a defense?

Author and scholar Wayne Grudem described:

> Scripture frequently affirms the fact that there will be a great final judgment of believers and unbelievers. They will stand

before the judgment seat of Christ in resurrected bodies and hear his proclamation of their eternal destiny.

The final judgment is vividly portrayed in John's vision in Revelation:

> Then I saw a great white throne and him who sat upon it; from his presence earth and sky fled away, and no place was found for them. And I saw the dead, great and small, standing before the throne, and books were opened. Also another book was opened, which is the book of life. And the dead were judged by what was written in the books, by what they had done. And the sea gave up the dead in it, death and hades gave up the dead in them, and all were judged by what they had done. Then death and hades were thrown into the lake of fire. This is the second death, the lake of fire; and if anyone's name was not found written in the book of life, he was thrown into the lake of fire. (Rev. 20:11–15)

Many other passages teach this final judgment. Paul tells the Greek philosophers in Athens that God "Now . . . commands all men everywhere to repent, because he has fixed a day on which he will judge the world in righteousness by a man whom he has appointed, and of this he has given assurance to all men by raising him from the dead" (Acts 17:30–31).[112] Similarly, Paul talks about "the day of wrath when God's righteous judgment will be revealed"

---

112. It is interesting that Paul proclaimed eternal judgment to unbelieving Gentiles who had little if any knowledge of the teachings of the Old Testament. Paul also argued about "future judgment" (Acts 24:25) before another unbeliever, the Roman governor Felix. In both cases Paul apparently realized that the brute fact that a day of accountability before God was coming to all men would give to his hearers a sobering realization that their eternal destiny was at stake as they listened to him preach about Jesus.

> Peter reminds us that God's
> judgments have been carried out
> periodically and with certainty . . .

(Rom. 2:5). Other passages speak clearly of a coming day of judgment (see Matt. 10:15; 11:22, 24; 12:36; 25:31–46; 1 Cor. 4:5; Heb. 6:2; 2 Peter 2:4; Jude 6; et al.).

This final judgment is the culmination of many precursors in which God rewarded righteousness or punished unrighteousness throughout history. While he brought blessing and deliverance from danger to those who were faithful to him, including Abel, Noah, Abraham, Isaac, Jacob, Moses, David, and the faithful among the people of Israel, he also from time to time brought judgment on those who persisted in disobedience and unbelief: his judgments included the flood, the dispersion of the people from the tower of Babel, the judgments on Sodom and Gomorrah, and continuing judgments throughout history, both on individuals (Rom. 1:18–32) and on nations (Isa. 13–23; et al.) who persisted in sin. Moreover, in the unseen spiritual realm he brought judgment on angels who sinned (2 Peter 2:4). Peter reminds us that God's judgments have been carried out periodically and with certainty, and this reminds us that a final judgment is yet coming, for "the Lord knows how to rescue the godly from trial, and to keep the unrighteousness under punishment until the day of judgment, and especially those who indulge in the lust of defiling passion and despise authority" (2 Peter 2:9–10). . . .

Unbelievers will be judged. It is clear that all unbelievers will stand before Christ for judgment, for this judgment includes "the dead, great and small" (Rev. 20:12), and

Paul says that "on the day of wrath when God's righteous judgment will be revealed," "he will render to every man according to his works . . . for those who are factious and do not obey the truth, but obey wickedness, there will be wrath and fury" (Rom. 2:5–7). This judgment of unbelievers will include degrees of punishment, for we read that the dead were judged "by what they had done" (Rev. 20:12, 13), and this judgment according to what people had done must therefore involve an evaluation of the works that people have done.[113, 114]

It is only by the blood of Jesus, the perfect Lamb that was slain, that I will hear "not guilty" on the Day of Judgment. My defense is found in him. All of us, great and small—every man, woman, and child—will stand before God as he examines our lives and our deeds done on earth. Why would anyone want to stand before God on this day without Jesus by his or her side?

FOR FURTHER THOUGHT

Can you think of things in your life for which you will need Jesus' defense as you stand before God on Judgment Day?

---

113. The fact that there will be degrees of punishment for unbelievers according to their works does not mean that unbelievers can ever do enough good to merit God's approval or earn salvation, for salvation only comes as a free gift to those who trust in Christ: "Whoever believes in him is not condemned, but whoever does not believe stands condemned already because they have not believed in the name of God's one and only Son" (John 3:18).

114. Wayne Grudem, *Heaven and Hell: A Zondervan Digital Short* (Grand Rapids: Zondervan, 2012), 31–97. Kindle Edition.

WHAT WILL HAPPEN TO THE **WICKED** AND THE **RIGHTEOUS** ON JUDGMENT DAY?

> And the Lord replied, "If I find fifty righteous people in Sodom, I will spare the entire city for their sake."
>
> **—GENESIS 18:26 NLT**

We see in this Bible story that Abraham, a man of faith, is very concerned for the welfare of God's people. He is speaking to God on their behalf. He is asking God to save them when he brings judgment and justice to the cities of Sodom and Gomorrah. When I read this story I can't help but feel convicted: Am I that concerned about God's justice? Do I care what happens to the righteous and the wicked on Judgment Day? If you are like most, this is probably not something you spend much time thinking about.

Missionary and author Douglas Jacoby wrote:

People of faith ought to be deeply concerned with God's justice. We should be bothered to think that most of the world may not make it at the last day. It should bother us even more to think that God may have got it wrong—that some folks got a raw deal and that a cosmic miscarriage of justice is in the wings. Ever since Abraham (Genesis 18:25) and Lot (2 Peter 2:7), men and women of faith have wrestled with this issue. . . .

The passage on the narrow gate, Matthew 7:13–14, is probably more familiar than a similar passage in the third Gospel, but the essence is the same.

> Someone asked him, "Lord, are only a few people going to be saved?"
>
> He said to them, "Make every effort to enter through the narrow door, because many, I tell you, will try to enter and will not be able to" (Luke 13:23–24).

We presume that the Lord knows who will be saved, and the percentages are not our concern. Notice how Jesus answered the man. He does not give a yes or a no. The answer is not a piece of information, but an imperative to the heart. He says, "Make every effort . . ." How many people are doing that—truly putting God first? Am I doing that? . . .

There are two doors (or gates) because there are two paths. We might prefer a third (more comfortable, more balanced) route, but this is not offered. In fact, the theme of two paths runs through every book of the Bible. You find it in Psalm 1 and the many other psalms that contrast the way of the righteous and the way of the wicked. It's in Acts (the Christians were called "The Way"). It's all over the Proverbs. . . .

One of my favorite passages touching on the narrow road is Isaiah 35:8 (NASB).

> *A highway will be there, a roadway,*
> *And it will be called the Highway of Holiness.*
> *The unclean will not travel on it,*
> *But it will be for him who walks that way,*
> *And fools will not wander on it.*

The Lord calls us to holy living. To be spiritual, not worldly (James 4:4; 1 John 2:15–17). To resist temptation in all its forms—egocentrism, materialism, sexual sin, laziness, drunkenness, bitterness . . . The New Testament includes some 30 lists of sins, so I am always stunned when people say the Bible isn't all that specific or that sin is whatever you think is wrong for you (but not necessarily for them).

And yet holiness is more than just resisting sin. Christ calls us to follow him—something active, not passive. We are called to be passionate, to catch fire for him (Romans 12:11; Revelation 3:14–20). If you commit yourself to the highway of holiness, there will be pushback.[115]

Ultimately, it is up to the Judge of the whole earth to decide who goes to heaven and who goes to hell. We see that the prayers and the words of one righteous man, Abraham, resulted in God's mercy on people in the midst of judgment. Because of Abraham, a righteous man named Lot was saved (Gen. 29:19) when Sodom and Gomorrah were destroyed. In the end, we must trust that both God's mercy and his judgment will rule with him on Judgment Day.

FOR FURTHER THOUGHT

How can you intercede—or stand in the gap—on behalf of someone who needs to experience God's mercy? Or maybe you currently need to experience God's mercy?

---

115. Douglas A. Jacoby, *What's the Truth About Heaven and Hell?* (Eugene, OR: Harvest House Publishers, 2013), 165–167.

Unknown Artist;
The Punishment of the Damned;
19th c.

"Hell is just a frame of mind."

— Christopher Marlowe, *Doctor Faustus*

"Truth by definition excludes."

— Ravi Zacharias

"But our emotions are a fluctuating, unreliable guide to truth and must not be exalted to the place of supreme authority in determining it."

— John Stott

"To terrify children with the image of hell, to consider women an inferior creation—is that good for the world?"

— Christopher Hitchens

"I hold it to be the inalienable right of anybody to go to hell in his own way."

— Robert Frost

"Are men and women going to allow the Word of God to sit in judgment on their puny minds, or are they going to make their puny minds the judges of the Word of God?"

— Alistair Begg

"I find your lack of faith disturbing."
—Darth Vader

"God keeps no half-way house. It's either heaven or hell for you and me."
—Billy Sunday

For if God did not spare angels when they sinned, but sent them to hell, putting them in chains of darkness to be held for judgment; if he did not spare the ancient world when he brought the flood on its ungodly people, but protected Noah, a preacher of righteousness, and seven others; if he condemned the cities of Sodom and Gomorrah by burning them to ashes, and made them an example of what is going to happen to the ungodly; and if he rescued Lot, a righteous man, who was distressed by the depraved conduct of the lawless (for that righteous man, living among them day after day, was tormented in his righteous soul by the lawless deeds he saw and heard)—if this is so, then the Lord knows how to rescue the godly from trials and to hold the unrighteous for punishment on the day of judgment. This is especially true of those who follow the corrupt desire of the flesh and despise authority.

—2 PETER 2:4–10

WILL A **LOVING GOD** REALLY **CONDEMN** PEOPLE TO HELL?

God will repay each person according to what they have done.

—ROMANS 2:6

When I am having a moral dilemma and want some good advice, I always go to my most intelligent and trusted friends. I wouldn't go to my casual friends who don't seem to take anything in life seriously and focus only on football.

What does it mean to be a thoughtful Christian? J. I. Packer, a well-respected leader in Christian circles, wrote, "The problem of individual human destiny has always pressed hard upon thoughtful Christians who take the Bible seriously." He understands that the reality of hell is not something to take casually. Below, Packer responds to a popular doctrine called universalism, which argues that all people will eventually be saved. Packer discusses three key aspects of hell that he believes Scripture confirms:

(1) The *reality of hell* as a state of eternal, destructive punishment, in which God's judgment for sin is directly experienced;

(2) The *certainty of hell* for all who choose it by rejecting Jesus Christ and his offer of eternal life; and

(3) The *justice of hell* as an appropriate divine judgment upon humanity for our lawless and cruel deeds.

It was, to be sure, hell-deserving sinners whom Jesus came to save. All who put their trust in him may know themselves forgiven, justified, and accepted forever—and thus delivered from the wrath to come. But what of those who lack this living faith—those who are hypocrites in the church; or "good pagans" who lived before Christ's birth; or those who, through no fault of their own, never heard the Christian message, or who met it only in an incomplete and distorted form? Or what of those who lived in places where Christianity was a capital offense, or who suffered from ethno-nationalistic or sociocultural conditioning against the faith, or who were so resentful of Christians for hurting them in some way that they were never emotionally free for serious thoughts about Christian truth? Are they all necessarily lost?

The universalistic idea that all people will eventually be saved by grace is a comforting belief. It relieves anxiety about the destiny of pagans, atheists, devotees of non-Christian religions, victims of post-Christian secularity—the millions of adults who never hear the gospel and millions of children who die before they can understand it. All sensitive Christians would like to embrace universalism. It would get us off a very painful hook.

However, no biblical passage unambiguously asserts universal final salvation, and some speak very explicitly about the lost-ness of the lost. Universalism is a theological speculation that discounts the meaning of these New Testament passages in favor of what Universalists claim to be thrust of New Testament thinking: that is, that God's retributive justice toward humanity is always a disciplinary expression of love that ultimately wins them salvation.

It would be nice to believe that, but Scripture nowhere suggests it when speaking of judgment, and the counter arguments seem overwhelmingly cogent. Universalism ignores the constant biblical stress on the decisiveness and finality of this life's decisions for determining eternal destiny.

"God 'will give to each person according to what he has done.' To those who by persistence in doing good seek glory, honor and immortality, he will give eternal life. But for those who are self-seeking and who reject the truth and follow evil, there will be wrath and anger. There will be trouble and distress for every human being who does evil . . . but glory, honor, and peace for everyone who does good . . . For God does not show favoritism" (Romans 2:6–11). This is Paul affirming God's justice according to the classic definition of justice, as giving everyone his or her due. All Scripture speaks this way.

Universalism condemns Christ himself, who warned people to flee hell at all costs. If it were true that all humanity will ultimately be saved from hell, he would have to have been either *incompetent* (ignorant that all were going to be saved) or *immoral* (knowing, but concealing it, so as to *bluff* people into the kingdom through fear).

The Universalist idea of sovereign grace saving all non-believers after death raises new problems.

If God has the ability to bring all to faith eventually, why would he not do it in this life in every case where the gospel is known?

If it is beyond God's power to convert all who know the gospel here, on what grounds can we be sure that he will be able to do it hereafter?

The Universalist's doctrine of God cannot be made fully coherent.

Universalism, therefore, as a theory about destiny, will not work. This life's decisions must be deemed to be decisive. And thus, proclaiming the gospel to our fallen, guilty, and hell-bent fellows must be the first service we owe them in light of their first and basic need.[116]

In the midst of all of these so-called debates about hell, it is easy to lose sight of the one important thing: Jesus himself. May it be his life, his words, and his cross that we remember as we carefully think through these challenging doctrines.

FOR FURTHER THOUGHT
Are there some thoughtful Christians in your life with whom you could discuss these doctrines?

WHAT ARE SOME OF THE MAJOR OBJECTIONS TO THE DOCTRINE OF HELL?

Just as people are destined to die once, and after that to face judgment, so Christ was sacrificed once to take away the sins of many; and he will appear a second time, not to bear sin, but to bring salvation to those who are waiting for him.

—HEBREWS 9:27–28

---

116. J. I. Packer, "Dr. J. I. Packer Answers the Question 'Will A Loving God Really Condemn People to Hell?'" LifeCoach4God, August 16, 2013, http://verticallivingministries.com/2012/04/09/dr-j-i-packer-answers-the-question-will-a-loving-god-really-condemn-people-to-hell/.

What are some of your objections to the doctrine of hell? Can you explain why it is that you object to that particular aspect of hell? Can you quote Scripture and other theologians on the matter? In other words, have you done your research in order to know why you believe what you believe?

Below, Mark Driscoll, a popular author and pastor, interacts with some of the most common objections about hell: 1) A loving God wouldn't send billions of people to hell. 2) God is completely tolerant. 3) Eternal torment isn't fair punishment for people who sinned for just a few decades.

> In a very important sense God doesn't send anyone to hell. The only ones there are those who have rejected his revelation, choosing to suppress the truth he made plain to them. God made people in his image, after his likeness, with the power to say no and to reject the universal revelation of himself. Subsequently, sinners have no one to blame but themselves if they are damned.
>
> To get to hell someone must reject the God who shows them his goodness and out of love for all "gives to all mankind life and breath and everything"; reject the Spirit who "convicts the world concerning sin and righteousness and judgment"; and reject the crucified Son who said, "I, when I am lifted up from the earth, will draw all people to myself." Obviously, God has been exceedingly gracious to sinners.
>
> People who reject Jesus in this life will not rejoice in him after this life. Hell is only for

What are some of your objections to the doctrine of hell?

those who persistently reject the real God in favor of false gods. So in the end, people get to be with the god they love. To paraphrase C. S. Lewis, either people will say to God, "Thy will be done," or God will say to them, "Thy will be done." Not only is God loving, but he is also just. Heaven and hell are the result of his love and justice. . . .

People who judge God need to really consider if they would be more pleased if God were tolerant of everyone, including rapists, pimps, pedophiles, and even those who have sinned against them most heinously. The idea is completely absurd and unjust. Not everyone in hell is a rapist, of course, but everyone there chose sin over God throughout his or her entire life . . .

A loving God protects his children from sin and evil by separating them. In this way, God is a father who is tolerant of all who obey him and are safe for his children. But he is intolerant of those who sin against him and do evil to his children. Subsequently, God is intolerant in a way that is like our own cultural intolerances of those who drink and drive, steal, rape, and murder; we, too, demonstrate our intolerance by separating such people from society. To call such actions on God's part intolerant is shameful, because tolerance would denote both approval and support of evil. . . .

Today, though, it is becoming popular to hope that sinners will eventually repent and everyone will end up in heaven. This is universal reconciliation, the ancient view of Origen. However, there is not a shred of evidence for post-mortem repentance. The continual teaching of the Bible is that we die once and are then judged, without any second chance at salvation. As one clear example, Hebrews 9:27 says,

"It is appointed for man to die once, and after that comes judgment."[117]

Having objections to things that make us feel pain or discomfort is normal. In fact, if you had no objections to the doctrine of hell, I might wonder if you were a thinking and feeling person. The doctrine of hell is one that causes us to wrestle with our consciences and our moral and ethical choices. Ultimately, you must decide for yourself what you believe and why you believe it. There will only be one person speaking with God on Judgment Day and that one person is you.

FOR FURTHER THOUGHT

What doctrine on hell is the most difficult for you to accept and why?

WILL THE TORMENT OF HELL LAST FOREVER?

As [Jesus] approached Jerusalem and saw the city, he wept over it.

—LUKE 19:41

There are "two sides to every story" and "two sides to every coin," or so the sayings go. My grandmother had a different expression: "There are two sides and then there's the truth—

---

117. Mark Driscoll, "To Hell with Hell?" *Resurgence: A Ministry of Mars Hill Church*, August 16, 2013, http://theresurgence.com/2011/03/14/to-hell-with-hell.

For hundreds of years, Christians have debated ideas about hell including how long it will last.

God's truth." I think my grandmother was wise.

While we may have our perspectives and our debates here on earth, none of us know the whole story. Only God knows the truth.

For hundreds of years, Christians have debated ideas about hell including how long it will last. Stanley J. Grenz, professor of theology at Carey/Regent College and Northern Baptist Theological Seminary, guides us through different points of view, including annihilation (or the belief that God will simply destroy the souls of unbelievers):

> The traditional teaching of the church—that the lost will suffer unending conscious torment in hell—has repeatedly been challenged by "universalists" since the third century. They believe that in the end, all will be saved. After the Reformation, a third viewpoint, "annihilationism" emerged as a minority position—for example, in the 1660 confession of the General Baptists, and among the Seventh-day Adventists and several other evangelical groups in the nineteenth century. Since 1960, several prominent British evangelicals, as well as Canadian theologian Clark Pinnock, have embraced this view. John Stott has likewise expressed sympathy for annihilationism while choosing to remain "agnostic" on the question.
>
> One key difference between universalists and annihilationists is that annihilationists agree with traditionalists

that many will indeed be lost eternally. By this, however, they mean that the unsaved will cease to exist for all eternity. They argue that because eternal torment serves no remedial purpose, the traditional concept of hell paints a portrait of God as a vindictive despot incompatible with the loving Father revealed in Jesus. Further, they claim that the presence of people in hell throughout eternity contradicts the Christian truth that Christ has conquered every evil foe and God will reconcile all things in Christ.

Some annihilationists who are better described as holding to "conditional immortality" claim the idea of eternal conscious punishment depends on the Greek concept of the immortality of the soul, which they say is wrongly read back into the Bible. The Bible teaches, they argue, that we are dependent on God for life, so only through participation in Christ's resurrection are the saved given immortality.

Annihilationists believe the Bible teaches that the end of the wicked is destruction, not eternal torment. Building from the Old Testament (Ps. 37; Mal. 4), they point to how Jesus declared that the wicked will be cast into the smoldering garbage heap of Gehenna (Matt. 5:30), where they will be burned up (Matt. 3:10–12) and destroyed in both body and soul (Matt. 10:28). Similarly, Paul spoke of the fate of the lost as death (Rom. 6:23) and destruction (1 Cor. 3:17). Peter also used such language (2 Peter 2), likening the destruction of the ungodly to the burning of Sodom and Gomorrah. And John anticipated the wicked being consumed

> Annihilationists believe the Bible teaches that the end of the wicked is destruction, not eternal torment.

in the lake of fire, which he called "the second death" (Rev. 20:14–15).

Whatever its appeal, the annihilationist position contains substantive problems. One is the biblical assertion that the wicked will suffer an "eternal" fate. Annihilationists argue that the word *eternal* refers to the permanence of the results of judgment and not to the duration of the act of punishment. Many Scripture passages, however, say more than this. Biblical writers use the word *eternal* to refer not only to the punishment of the lost but also to the bliss of the righteous (Matt. 25:46), suggesting a parallel that goes beyond the permanence of the pronounced judgment. The unending joy of the redeemed stands in contrast to the unending torment of the reprobate.

Also, several New Testament texts indicate that the lost will suffer varying degrees of punishment. Jesus declared that those who have received greater opportunities for belief will suffer more severe condemnation (Matt. 10:15; 11:20–24; Luke 12:47–48). While many annihilationists believe in different degrees of torment before extinction, they anticipate only one ultimate destiny for all the wicked, an undifferentiated nonexistence. But can a righteous Judge pronounce the same sentence of destiny upon the most despicable villain of human history as upon the seemingly moral pagan? Also, doesn't passing out of existence trivialize the seriousness of the choices we make in life and the importance of our response to God's loving offer of community?

In sum, yes, some evangelical theologians affirm annihilationism, but it is important to keep in mind that annihilationists affirm several aspects of the traditional view. This issue, therefore, should not be lumped in with the more substantial debate over universalism, which denies a final judgment altogether. The debate raised by annihilationists reminds us of the difficulties that arise whenever we attempt to pinpoint the eternal situation of the lost. Just as we cannot envision what conscious bliss will mean to the saved in their resurrection bodies, so also we do not know exactly what eternal punishment will be like. Finally, the controversy surrounding the nature of eternal damnation will serve a positive purpose if it leads us to realize that we ought never to speak about the fate of the lost without tears in our eyes.[118]

The debates have continued through the years with Christians landing on both sides of the coin. Ultimately, in his infinite wisdom, God has not given us all the answers and there is much more we want to know. He has provided us with the ability to have conversations and to search our own hearts. But that's not all. He asks us to follow Christ and to spend eternity with him as opposed to any awful alternative.

FOR FURTHER THOUGHT

Do you value God's justice as well as his mercy?

---

118. Stanley J. Grenz, "Directions: Is Hell Forever?" *Christianity Today* 42, no. 11: 92 (September 3, 2011).

IS HELL A PLACE OF **ANNIHILATION,** ETERNAL **TORMENT,** OR NEITHER?

If your hand causes you to stumble, cut it off. It is better for you to enter life maimed than with two hands to go into hell, where the fire never goes out.

—MARK 9:43

Recently the world got pretty stirred up about the Guantanamo Bay detainees—international terrorists who were imprisoned indefinitely, some without trial. Some were tortured for information and confessions. So if that makes so many people upset, what about the thought of God eternally detaining and punishing people? Does that jive with our belief that God is a God of love? Throughout the centuries, some Christians have wondered if there might be a doctrine called "annihilationism." That is, rather than condemn someone to hell for eternity, might God simply end their existence?

Annihilationism is a belief that was popularized by a Texas lawyer named Edward Fudge. In response, Robert Yarbrough guides us through different points of view, including annihilation or the destruction of the soul:

> Houston lawyer Edward W. Fudge has become well-known
> for advocating the view . . . that when the wicked die, their

punishment is eternal death rather than eternal torment. This view is called conditional immortality or annihilationism. Fudge writes:

> The fact is that the Bible does not teach the traditional view of final punishment. Scripture nowhere suggests that God is an eternal torturer. It never says the damned will writhe in ceaseless torment or that the glories of heaven will forever be blighted by the screams from hell. The idea of conscious everlasting torment was a grievous mistake, a horrible error, a gross slander against the heavenly Father, whose character we truly see in the life of Jesus of Nazareth.[119]

Some of Fudge's language may be set aside as heated rhetoric. The historic view does not see God as "an eternal torturer" but rather as a righteous judge (see Rom. 3:5–6). Heaven will not "forever be blighted by the screams from hell," but will rather be a place with "no more death or mourning or crying or pain, for the old order of things has passed away" (Rev. 21:4). Without giving all of the details, Scripture promises that hell's woes will not mar heaven's blessedness.

More importantly, to call belief in conscious everlasting punishment "a grievous mistake, a horrible error, a gross slander against the heavenly Father" is a risky charge in light of the words of Jesus on hell. Jesus speaks clearly about the "traditional" view that Fudge associates with slander of God.

In order to refute Fudge's view, let's look at a couple of key passages in which he offers an interpretation very different from the traditional one.

---

119. Edward W. Fudge and Robert A. Peterson, *Two Views of Hell* (Downers Grove, IL: InterVarsity Press, 2000), 20; see also 82.

"Do not be afraid of those who kill the body but cannot kill the soul. Rather, be afraid of the One who can destroy both soul and body in hell" (Matt. 10:28). Fudge stresses that "kill" and "destroy" are parallel, and he understands "destroy" to mean annihilate. So Jesus' warning is to fear God because he can make both soul and body cease to exist any longer.[120]

However, it makes better sense to understand Jesus' warning as it has historically been understood. Matthew 10 is about Jesus' sending out the Twelve. They will face danger, treachery, and things like flogging (10:17). They will be tempted to be cowardly rather than face pain or even death. But there is a second death more fearful than any earthly end. God is able to inflict an unending misery on the whole person, "soul and body." We say "unending" for two reasons.

First, Jesus in a similar passage calls this affliction "eternal" (remember the discussion above), and there is no compelling reason to interpret a death Jesus calls eternal elsewhere as temporary here.

Second, "destroy" in the New Testament can sometimes refer to enduring torment. For instance, the unclean spirits who ask whether Jesus will "destroy" them (Mark 1:24; Luke 4:34) are clearly not afraid of death or even temporary torment. Rather, they fear that Jesus might begin the "forever and ever" torment that the book of Revelation says is the destiny of the devil and all those loyal to him (Rev. 14:11), including unclean spirits.

Taken alone, this one passage may be inconclusive, however. So let's look at another one. "It is better for you to enter the kingdom of God with one eye than to have two eyes and

120. Ibid., 43–44.

be thrown into hell, where 'the worms that eat them do not die, and the fire is not quenched'" (Mark 9:47–48).

In dealing with this verse, Fudge sticks to his guns: "The devouring worm is aided by unquenchable fire that cannot be put out and that therefore continues to destroy until nothing remains." He appeals to a reading of Isaiah 66:24, which Jesus quotes in this passage, that sees in the worm and fire imagery corpses that decompose or are burned into oblivion.

This is an unlikely interpretation of Isaiah's meaning. For one thing, the logic is strained. A fire that "continues to destroy until nothing remains" is not unquenchable; instead, it goes out after everything is burned up.[121]

If someone focuses solely on the love of God, it is understandable that the doctrine of hell becomes difficult to hold. And though God is love, he is much more—including holy and just. God is not an imperfect, earthly government that holds prisoners without trial. He will not punish for pleasure or without cause. I may not have all the answers, but I know I can trust God's judgment; a person's eternal destiny in hell will be both fair and impartial.

FOR FURTHER THOUGHT

Do you tend to focus more on God's holiness or his love? If you focus exclusively on his love, how might your view of God be incomplete?

---

121. Timothy Keller, R. Albert Mohler Jr., J. I. Packer, and Robert Yarbrough, *Is Hell for Real or Does Everyone Go to Heaven?* (Grand Rapids: Zondervan, 2011), 30–32.

HOW CAN THE TRUTH ABOUT HELL AFFECT OUR LIVES TODAY?

"Hell is empty and all the devils are here."

—William Shakespeare

"The hottest place in Hell is reserved for those who remain neutral in times of great moral conflict."

—Martin Luther King Jr.

"Religion is for people who are scared to go to hell. Spirituality is for people who have already been there."

—Bonnie Raitt

"The concept of Hell might really keep you out of trouble."

—Sarah Silverman, *The Bedwetter: Stories of Courage, Redemption, and Pee*

"You can all go to hell; I will go to Texas."

—David Crockett

"Jesus didn't speak of hell so that we could study, debate and write books about it. He gave us these passages so that we would live holy lives."

—Francis Chan, *Erasing Hell*

f a righteous person turns from their righteousness and commits sin, they will die for it; because of the sin they have committed they will die. But if a wicked person turns away from the wickedness they have committed and does what is just and right, they will save their life. Because they consider all the offenses they have committed and turn away from them, that person will surely live; they will not die. . . .

Therefore, you Israelites, I will judge each of you according to your own ways, declares the Sovereign LORD. Repent! Turn away from all your offenses; then sin will not be your downfall. Rid yourselves of all the offenses you have committed, and get a new heart and a new spirit. Why will you die, people of Israel? For I take no pleasure in the death of anyone, declares the Sovereign LORD. Repent and live!

—EZEKIEL 18:26–28, 30–32

SHOULD ALL CHRISTIANS TALK ABOUT HEAVEN AND HELL?

> We are therefore Christ's ambassadors, as though God were making his appeal through us.
>
> —2 CORINTHIANS 5:20

Is it necessary for a tornado siren to be able to actually sound? Would you consider a road construction flagger to be doing his job if he hid his signs in the weeds by the roadside and slept in a lawn chair? What might happen if a pilot car took down the "oversize load" signs and turned off the yellow caution light? In the same way, is it necessary for Christians to talk about hell? What do you think?

Our actions and behavior in the world give voice to a faith that is often unseen. Actions are evidence of our faith, are they not? If you're like most Christians, then you would probably rather stick to talking about heaven and completely skip over hell, but what's the good news if there is nothing to be saved from?

Brian Jones, pastor and author of *Hell Is Real (But I Hate to Admit It)*, has explained that Christians are ambassadors for Christ:

> Ambassadors in Paul's time were people sent to foreign countries to speak on behalf of their king. Their responsibilities were identical to what they are today:
>
> - Move to a foreign country.
>
> - Learn the language.
>
> - Respect the people and culture.
>
> - Don't say or do anything that reflects poorly on the king.
>
> - Communicate the king's message to foreign dignitaries.
>
> - Press for a decision.
>
> - Don't burn any bridges.

As Christ's ambassadors to nonbelievers within our circles of influence, that list pretty much sums up our part in the evangelism process. Our job is to build authentic relationships by learning their language (both literally and

> Being an ambassador,
> however, is more than just
> presenting information.

culturally), showing respect, being mindful of how our actions reflect upon Christ's cause, and when the opportunity presents itself, speaking "as though God were making his appeal through us" (2 Cor. 5:20). Being an ambassador, however, is more than just presenting information. Ambassadors aren't sent to foreign countries because the sending country likes to keep other countries updated on their affairs. Matters of crucial importance are at stake, and decisions that affect national security must be made.

Ambassadors deliver information and then call for a decision. The reason you can't make excuses about not evangelizing is because you are needed to press for this decision! Jesus didn't say, "Go ye therefore and build religious billboards" or "Go ye therefore and hide evangelism tracts in public restrooms so when people have to relieve themselves they'll find out about me." He said, "You will be my witnesses" (Acts 1:8). That means we're called to make human to human contact. What your nonbelieving friends need is a Christian they trust who will clear his or her throat, look them in the eyes, explain the story of Jesus, and then ask them if they're ready to reconcile with God.

Paul wrote, "We implore you on Christ's behalf: Be reconciled to God" (2 Cor. 5:20). That's why God needs you. You may be the only ambassador of Jesus your nonbelieving friends will ever encounter. Do you understand that?

The issue is not *whether or not* you are Christ's ambassador to them—*you are.* God already decided that. The question is whether or not you are a good ambassador. Make all the excuses you want, God sent you into your circle of influence to do a job, and there is no plan B if you don't complete the job.

Jesus isn't going to send in the angels if you drop the ball. God isn't going to speak audibly to your friends to give them the opportunity to respond in faith to what He did in Jesus. Information about how to become a Christian will not spontaneously appear in your coworker's brain by the power of the Holy Spirit. The heavens aren't going to open up. The saints of old aren't going to come rushing in at the last second.

For whatever reason, God in His infinite wisdom (or audacity) chose to work through us to complete His ministry of reconciliation. What that means is you're the only plan God has.

You are the ministry of reconciliation.

Let that sink in.

You're it. You're responsible. . . .

Every time we help someone walk across the line of faith, we get a front-row seat to watch an astonishing act of creation. But unlike the acts of creation detailed in the book of Genesis, this creation happens in the heart, unseen by human eyes. But it's just as miraculous nonetheless.

That's why evangelism is a privilege. It's not just a *have to*, but a *get to*. Can you believe that God in His gracious compassion, given all that we put Him through because of our sin, turns around and allows us to participate in His effort to reclaim human

Jesus isn't going to send in the angels if you drop the ball.

lives? It's a stupendous act of grace. Who are we, creatures deserving God's full wrath because of our wickedness, to deserve such a privilege? It's astonishing to consider. The God of the universe not only refuses to count our sin against us, but also picks us up, brushes us off, looks us in the eye, and tells us that He needs us.[122]

I know it can be scary to open your mouth and talk about these things that are beyond our comprehension, but God says, "Open wide your mouth and I will fill it" (Ps. 81:10). Whenever I have had the courage to open my mouth, he truly has given me words to speak. And he has been faithful to fill me with love for the people to whom I was speaking.

FOR FURTHER THOUGHT

What excuses do you make about why you can't discuss heaven and hell with the people in your life?

---

122. Brian Jones, *Hell Is Real (But I Hate to Admit It)* (Colorado Springs, CO: David C. Cook, 2011), 166–169.

HOW MUCH RESPONSIBILITY DO CHRISTIANS HAVE FOR OTHER PEOPLE'S SALVATION?

> Preach the word; be prepared in season and out of season; correct, rebuke and encourage—with great patience and careful instruction.
>
> **—2 TIMOTHY 4:2**

I think we have gotten off track in the American church with the professionalization of preachers. I've noticed this steady movement away from every Christian believer's call and charge to preach the Word to others, instead leaving the responsibility to those on stage and up front.

As we go and live out our Christian lives among nonbelievers, what exactly are we responsible for? Brian Jones explained:

> Our words can be responsible for propelling another person headlong toward the gates of hell. It's one thing not to share the gospel with someone. That's an error of omission. But potentially misdirecting someone through wrong teaching, possibly for all eternity—that's a heavy responsibility to lay on someone, especially for those who are still brand-new Christians trying to figure out this whole Christianity thing for themselves. But it's true. As Christians, not only can we save ourselves and our hearers by what we teach, we can

damn ourselves and our hearers as well. But there's something even worse than that. Christians can negatively impact what another Christian believes. We can influence another Christian to stop believing in hell. The end result of that action is much worse than directing one non-Christian to hell. When one Christian influences another to stop believing in hell, it has ripple effects throughout that person's life. As John Mott wrote, "The greatest hindrances to the evangelization of the world are those within the church."[123] If you rob a Christian of apocalyptic urgency, you lose every single non-Christian that person could have reached in his or her lifetime. Instead of becoming a Christian who multiplies thirty, sixty, or a hundred times, like Jesus talked about in the parable of the sower (Matt. 13:23), this person will become a believer whose influence is metaphorically buried in the ground. . . .

Our spiritually tolerant culture has indoctrinated us to believe that "God is a loving God." While it is true that God is love, He is equally a God of justice. Because God is a God of justice, He is just as concerned with inflicting judgment upon His creation when it sins as He is with loving it. This is absolutely counter to what many Christians believe, but this is what the Bible plainly teaches. . . .

Who will this just God punish? It's very clear: those who have offended His holy nature by their sin and failed to respond to His gracious offer of forgiveness through His Son, Jesus. Current estimates put the worldwide population at roughly seven billion people. Since a little more than two billion people claim to adhere to the Christian faith, this leaves five billion people alive today who are headed toward

123. John R. Mott, *The Evangelization of the World in This Generation* (BiblioLife, 2009) (New York: Student Volunteer Movement, 1905), 49.

punishment. . . . The worst part about this tragedy is that God will withdraw from those being punished—they will not feel His presence. After death all non-Christians will exist in a place where everything that God is—hope, love, goodness, joy, etc.—is completely absent. . . .

Everyday Christians have an opportunity to influence not three million viewers but two or three non-Christians—over a working lunch, or while standing in line for a concert, or during a Bible study. If we fail to present the biblical facts about a non-Christian's spiritual status before God, we have failed in our most basic duty as Christ followers. The apostle Paul's warning in 2 Timothy 4:1–5 stands as a sober reminder that there will always be some Christians who are afraid to tell the truth. In the presence of God and of Christ Jesus, who will judge the living and the dead, and in view of his appearing and his kingdom, I give you this charge: "Preach the word; be prepared in season and out of season; correct, rebuke and encourage—with great patience and careful instruction. For the time will come when people will not put up with sound doctrine. Instead, to suit their own desires, they will gather around them a great number of teachers to say what their itching ears want to hear. They will turn their ears away from the truth and turn aside to myths. But you, keep your head in all situations, endure hardship, do the work of an evangelist, discharge all the duties of your ministry."

If there ever was a time that passage needed to be understood, felt, and obeyed, it's today.[124]

Sharing the good news, and the bad, is not just for the paid pastors and those in ministry. It is for every man, woman, and

---

124. Brian Jones, *Hell Is Real (But I Hate to Admit It)* (Colorado Springs, CO: David C. Cook, 2011), 74–75, 79–81.

child. As we go about our lives, I hope we can be mindful of our witness in the world, taking every opportunity given to us to share the hope that we have in Jesus.

FOR FURTHER THOUGHT

Are there ways that you can prepare yourself to share the good news, or the gospel, with someone?

HOW CAN CHRISTIANS START CONVERSATIONS ABOUT HELL?

> Why do you stare at us as if by our own power or godliness we had made this man walk? The God of Abraham, Isaac and Jacob, the God of our fathers, has glorified his servant Jesus.
>
> **—ACTS 3:12–13**

As Christians, if we're honest, we'll admit that we can be embarrassed by street evangelists, televangelists, and the people with gospel messages on cardboard signs. Most of us have no idea how to start a conversation about a topic as tough as hell, and since it doesn't come up in casual conversation, it's easy to avoid altogether. During my lifetime, I've had probably just a handful of deep conversations about hell. For those of us outside of "professional" ministry, how do we bring it up? How does God want us to speak about him and to represent him in this world that he so loves?

Maybe it isn't so much that we need to start a conversation about hell, as it is that we need to lead lives that "provoke the question" to which the gospel is the answer. Bryant Myers, seminary professor and former World Vision practitioner, explained it this way:

> The book of Acts describes the evangelism and growth of the early church. Examining these stories reveals an interesting pattern. Evangelism, the saying of the gospel, is often the second not the first act.
>
> When Peter gives his first public statement of the gospel, we are told 3,000 believers were added that day. Yet his sermon was spontaneous. He begins it by saying, "let me explain this to you." What was the "this" that needed explaining? The fact that the people of Jerusalem could hear the disciples praising God, "speaking in his own language." This powerful act of the Holy Spirit made the people "utterly amazed" and so demanded an explanation. Peter's message was in response to a question asked by the crowd.
>
> The second articulation of the gospel in Acts follows a similar pattern. After Peter healed the crippled beggar at the temple gate, a crowd gathers, astonished at the sight of the former cripple walking and praising God. Peter once again finds himself needing to clarify the situation. "Men of Israel, why does this surprise you? Why do you stare at us as if by our own power or godliness we had made this man walk? The God of Abraham, Isaac and Jacob, the God of our fathers, has glorified his servant Jesus" (Acts 3:12–13). Once again Peter's speech is in response to a question provoked by evidence of God's activity.

The same pattern emerges in the story of Stephen. His opportunity to share the gospel's recomposed history of Israel came about not by plan, but as a result of his being falsely accused because the Spirit "did great wonders and miraculous signs among the people" (Acts 6:8). As a result of Stephen's preaching in front of the Sanhedrin, a Pharisee named Saul heard the gospel for the first time.

Do you see the common frame? In each case, the gospel is proclaimed, not by intent or plan, but in response to a question provoked by God's activity in the community. There is an action demanding an explanation, and the gospel explains the action. As Newbigin put it: "Something has happened which makes people aware of a new reality, and therefore the question arises: What is this reality? The communication of the gospel is the answering of that question." . . .

God does evangelism through the Christian community, acting in ways that provoke questions among the people to which the good news of Jesus Christ is the answer . . . The people ask the questions as a result of witnessing something they do not expect or understand. The initiative lies with them. This avoids Paul Tillich's complaint that "it is wrong to throw answers, like stones, at the heads of those who haven't even asked a question." Second, the burden is on the Christians, not the people. If the people do not ask questions to which the gospel is the answer, we can no longer just say, "Their hearts were hardened," and walk away feeling good that we have witnessed to the gospel. Instead,

There is an action demanding an explanation, and the gospel explains the action.

we need to get down on our knees and ask God why our lives and our work are so similar to everyone else's that no one has raised a question related to what we believe. . . .

We must do our work and live our lives in a way that calls attention to the new Spirit that lives within us . . . We must seek a spirituality that makes our lives eloquent. Dorothy Day is reported to have admonished us to "live a life so mysterious that the only adequate explanation is the presence of a living, loving God."[125]

Does your life provoke any questions about God, about heaven and hell, from people? Are you extravagantly generous or uncharacteristically compassionate? Are there signs that you have been touched by an otherworldly love, a love that comes from the Spirit of God within you? I'm challenged to make my life "the only Bible that people may ever read." If this is so, what will my life communicate? Will it lead people away from the path of destruction and toward everlasting life? I sure hope so.

FOR FURTHER THOUGHT

What messages does your life communicate to the world around you?

---

125. Bryant L. Myers, *Provoking the Question: Uniting Christian Witness and Transformational Development* (Federal Way, WA: World Vision International, 2006), 7–11.

WHY DON'T MORE CHRISTIANS TALK ABOUT HELL?

> Always be prepared to give an answer to everyone who asks you to give the reason for the hope that you have.
>
> **—1 PETER 3:15**

What are some tough topics that you don't like to discuss? One of my tough topics is my feelings. In the past, when someone asked me, "How does that make you feel?" I would find myself changing the subject pretty quickly. Fortunately, I've gotten better at expressing my emotions with the help of some great friends and a very patient wife. While I'm a lot better than I was, it isn't a subject that comes naturally for me. Like me discussing my feelings, I think the topic of hell is one of those tough subjects for most Christians. We're quick to dodge and then change the subject. Why do you think that is?

Brian Jones wrote:

> Christians stop believing in hell because they allow the non-Christians around them to make them feel stupid for believing in it. In my experience, followers of Jesus can go in the blink of an eye from wholeheartedly believing in the need to save their friends from hell to believing "everybody goes to heaven" all because of something a non-Christian said to them. This has been going on for two thousand years. I want to help change that. . . .

The problem is that a Christian who believes in hell and believes people who don't accept Jesus will go there for eternity is never going to be accepted by his or her non-Christian friends. It's just not going to happen. Let's be honest—hell isn't one of those topics of conversation that gets us invited back to dinner parties. We're never going to have a conversation with a non-Christian over Chicken Cordon Bleu after which he will lean over and tell us, "You know, I just love it when you insinuate that I'm going to hell. Love it. Love it. *Love it.*"

Jesus warns us that if we truly believe what He teaches and live the life He calls us to live, the non-Christians around us won't accept us:

You will be hated by everyone because of me. (Matt. 10:22)

You will be hated by all nations because of me. (Matt. 24:9)

If the world hates you, keep in mind that it hated me first. (John 15:18)

Two thousand years of church history have validated Jesus' claims. Read any history book if you doubt His comments. Turn on any late-night talk show. Or flip on the radio. Our culture ridicules Christians who take the Bible seriously and calls them Jesus freaks. There's a reason the apostle Peter warned, "Do not be surprised at the fiery ordeal that has come on you to test you, as though something strange were happening to you" (1 Peter 4:12). If you truly live out your beliefs, non-Christians are going to think you're nuts. And they will tell you so. *To your face.* A lot.

Two thousand years of church history have validated Jesus' claims.

The only comforting thing about this is that it's nothing new. It's been going on for two thousand years.

Take the book of Hebrews, for example. We don't know a lot about the person who wrote it or the people who received it other than what we can discern from contextual clues. As we read the book, the first thing we discover is that the Christians who received the letter had once been valiant in the face of extreme persecution. Their plight gives us a firsthand look at the intense social pressure first-century Christians faced.

> Remember those earlier days after you had received the light, when you endured in a great conflict full of suffering. (Heb. 10:32)

> You suffered along with those in prison and joyfully accepted the confiscation of your property, because you knew that you yourselves had better and lasting possessions. (v. 34)

But despite their long-standing history of bravery in the face of unrelenting community pressure, something changed. Something caused them to lose their zeal; so much so that many of them stopped gathering together as believers.

> And let us consider how we may spur one another on toward love and good deeds, not giving up meeting together, as some are in the habit of doing. (vv. 24–25)

How did this happen? How did these Christians go from letting unbelievers confiscate their property just to show them that their faith was real to skipping church and watching TV evangelists? Something powerful and disturbing must have happened in their community. To me the culprit is found in one lethal word: *insult*. Sometimes you were publicly exposed to *insult* and persecution. (v. 33)[126]

There are so many reasons we avoid certain subjects, especially hell. We might be afraid that we'll look stupid, cruel, or narrow-minded. But as the author above said, we can learn from the brave example of some of the early Christians who did not back down when they were insulted, harmed, and killed for their faith.

FOR FURTHER THOUGHT

How can you prepare your heart and mind to talk about the tough subject of hell with someone who may need to discuss it?

IS IT WRONG TO **HOPE** THAT ALL **PEOPLE** MIGHT BE **SPARED** HELL?

This is good, and pleases God our Savior, who wants all people to be saved and to come to a knowledge of the truth.

—1 TIMOTHY 2:3–4

I have been thinking about this concept of hell a lot lately. Let's say that I've been wandering around in a dark, scary place and now I've found my way out. Is it wrong for me to hope that other

---

126. Brian Jones, *Hell Is Real (But I Hate to Admit It)* (Colorado Springs, CO: David C. Cook, 2011), 47–51.

> In the parable of the sheep and
> the goats, Jesus indicates that
> some will be condemned.

wanderers might find their way out too? Is it not the love of God inside of us that makes us want to return for the others and call out, "Hey! I've found the way out!"? Can we hope—dare we hope, as one theologian has so famously written—that all people might be saved from hell?

Avery Cardinal Dulles, an American-born Jesuit priest and cardinal of the Catholic Church, wrote:

> As we know from the Gospels, Jesus spoke many times about hell. Throughout his preaching, he holds forth two and only two final possibilities for human existence: the one being everlasting happiness in the presence of God, the other everlasting torment in the absence of God. He describes the fate of the damned under a great variety of metaphors: everlasting fire, outer darkness, tormenting thirst, a gnawing worm, and weeping and gnashing of teeth.
>
> In the parable of the sheep and the goats, Jesus indicates that some will be condemned. The Son of man says to the goats: "Depart from me, you cursed, into the eternal fire prepared for the devil and his angels" (Matthew 25:41). In the Gospel of John . . . Jesus is quoted as saying: "The hour is coming when all who are in the tombs will hear [the Father's] voice and come forth, those who have done good, to the resurrection of life, and those who have done evil, to the resurrection of judgment" (John 5:28–29).
>
> The apostles, understandably concerned, asked: "Lord, will those who are saved be few?" Without directly answering

their question Jesus replied: "Strive to enter by the narrow door; for many, I tell you, will seek to enter and not be able" (Luke 13:23–24) . . . In another parable, that of the wedding guest who is cast out for not wearing the proper attire, Jesus declares: "Many are called, but few are chosen" (Matthew 22:14). Taken in their obvious meaning, passages such as these give the impression that there is a hell, and that many go there; more, in fact, than are saved.

The most sophisticated theological argument against the conviction that some human beings in fact go to hell has been proposed by Hans Urs von Balthasar in his book *Dare We Hope "That All Men Be Saved?"* He rejects the ideas that hell will be emptied at the end of time and that the damned souls and demons will be reconciled with God. He also avoids asserting as a fact that everyone will be saved. But he does say that we have a right and even a duty to *hope* for the salvation of all, because it is not impossible that even the worst sinners may be moved by God's grace to repent before they die.[127] He concedes, however, that the opposite is also possible. Since we are able to resist the grace of God, none of us is safe. We must therefore leave the question speculatively open, thinking primarily of the danger in which we ourselves stand. . . .

Balthasar's position . . . does not undermine a healthy fear of being lost. But the position is at least adventurous. It runs against the obvious interpretation of the words of Jesus in the New Testament and against the dominant theological opinion down through the centuries, which maintains that some, and in fact very many, are lost.

---

127. Hans Urs von Balthasar, *Dare We Hope "That All Men Be Saved"?* (San Francisco: Ignatius Press,1986).

Vatican II declares that all people, even those who have never heard of Christ, receive enough grace to make their salvation possible. . . .

In a General Audience talk of July 28, 1999, [Pope John Paul II said]:

> Christian faith teaches that in taking the risk of saying "yes" or "no," which marks the (human) creature's freedom, some have already said no. They are the spiritual creatures that rebelled against God's love and are called demons (cf. Fourth Lateran Council). What happened to them is a warning to us: it is a continuous call to avoid the tragedy which leads to sin and to conform our life to that of Jesus who lived his life with a "yes" to God.
>
> Eternal damnation remains a possibility, but we are not granted, without special divine revelation, the knowledge of *whether or which* human beings are effectively involved in it. The thought of hell—and even less the improper use of biblical images—must not create anxiety or despair, but is a necessary and healthy reminder of freedom within the proclamation that the risen Jesus has conquered Satan, giving us the Spirit of God who makes us cry "Abba, Father!" (Romans 8:15; Galatians 4:6).[128]

Dulles concludes, "We have a right to hope and pray that all will be saved. The fact that something is highly improbable need not prevent us from hoping and praying that it will happen. According to the Catechism of the Catholic Church, 'In hope, the Church prays for "all men to be saved" (1 Timothy

128. Avery Cardinal Dulles, "The Population of Hell." *First Things: A Monthly Journal Of Religion & Public Life* no. 133: 36 (May 2003). Used by permission.

2:4).'[129] At another point the Catechism declares: 'The Church prays that no one should be lost.'"[130] Let us join with the world-wide church in praying such a prayer.

FOR FURTHER THOUGHT

Does the thought of people being lost stir up compassion in your heart and motivate you to pray?

129. "Catechism of the Catholic Church (CCC§1821)," *Vatican*, August 14, 2013, http://www.vatican.va/archive/ccc_css/archive/catechism/p3s1c1a7.htm.

130. "Catechism of the Catholic Church (CCC §1058)," *Vatican*, August 14, 2013, http://www.vatican.va/archive/ccc_css/archive/catechism/p123a12.htm.

AFTERWORD

Finding Our Way to Heaven

At the conclusion of this book, many readers may have one final question: *How can I be sure to secure eternal life in heaven and avoid hell?* Jesus provided the answer when he said two simple words: "Follow me" (John 1:43).

What does *following Jesus* mean? To follow Jesus is to embrace that he's alive, that his words matter, and that his priorities outweigh our own. Following Jesus is to do what he says and follow the path he has for us. It is putting aside our own interests, dreams, and ambitions in order to follow the course he has laid out for us.

Jesus said, "I am the light of the world. Whoever follows me will never walk in darkness, but will have the light of life" (John 8:12). By following Jesus, we travel a well-lit path that leads to heaven, a place where we will experience life to the fullest in the presence of God himself.

But can't there be another way? Can't we be the masters of our own lives, follow our own paths, and still find a home in heaven? Jesus' answer to that is straightforward:

- "Whoever does not take up their cross and follow me is not worthy of me" (Matt. 10:38).

- "Whoever wants to be my disciple must deny themselves and take up their cross and follow me" (Matt. 16:24).

We are either following him or we're not. We are either on his path or we aren't. We are either putting aside our own interests—dying to ourselves—or we aren't. Jesus is the only way to heaven: "I am the way and the truth and the life. No one comes to the Father except through me" (John 14:6).

Can a future in heaven be guaranteed? Yes, absolutely, yes. Jesus offers a clearly marked path with a definite destination—heaven, where we can enjoy the presence of God and life to the fullest. We can confidently follow Jesus' path because we know he has traveled it before us. He has marked it with his words that urge us forward: "Come, follow me."

APPENDIX

List of Bible Verses on Heaven and Hell

HEAVEN

What Is Heaven?

Deuteronomy 26:15	God's holy dwelling place
1 Kings 8:30	God's dwelling place
2 Chronicles 30:27	God's holy dwelling place
Psalm 11:4	God's holy temple, his throne
Psalm 20:6	God's heavenly sanctuary
Psalm 23:6	The house of the Lord
Psalm 33:13–14	God's dwelling place
Psalm 102:19–20	God's sanctuary
Ecclesiastes 5:2	Where God is
Isaiah 57:15	A high and holy place
Isaiah 63:15	God's lofty throne
Isaiah 66:1	God's throne
Zechariah 2:13	God's holy dwelling place
Matthew 6:9–13	God's kingdom
Matthew 7:13–15	Life
Matthew 18:18	Where things are bound and loosed
Matthew 25:34	The kingdom God prepared for us since the creation of the world
John 3:16	Eternal life
John 3:36	Eternal life
John 14:1–4	The Father's house
Acts 7:49	God's throne; Jesus' resting place
1 Corinthians 15:50	Kingdom of God
2 Corinthians 5:2–3	Our heavenly dwelling
2 Corinthians 5:8	Our home

Galatians 4:26	Heavenly Jerusalem
Colossians 1:3–6	Where hope is
Hebrews 11:15–16	Heavenly country; a city
Hebrews 12:22–24	Mount Zion; the city of the living God; the heavenly Jerusalem
Hebrews 13:14	An enduring city; the city to come
2 Peter 3:13	New heaven, new earth; where righteousness dwells
Revelation 2:7	Where the Tree of Life is; the paradise of God
Revelation 3:12	The city of God; the New Jerusalem
Revelation 3:21	Where God's throne is
Revelation 21:4–8	The Holy City; the New Jerusalem

What Does God Do in Heaven?

Deuteronomy 26:15	Blesses the people of Israel and the land
1 Kings 8:30	Listens to his people; forgives
2 Chronicles 30:27	Hears/listens
Nehemiah 9:27	Hears/listens; has compassion; delivers his people
Psalm 11:4	Watches over everyone on earth
Psalm 16:9–11	Fills his people with joy in his presence
Psalm 20:6	Answers his people
Psalm 33:13–14	Watches all people
Psalm 73:24–25	Guides his people
Psalm 102:19–20	Looks down on the earth; hears and releases the prisoners
Psalm 103:19	Rules his kingdom
Psalm 115:15	Blesses his people
Psalm 119:89	His Word stands firm
Psalm 121:1–2	Helps his people
Psalm 123:1	Sits enthroned
Psalm 136:26	Loves forever
Isaiah 6:2–4	Receives worship
Isaiah 49:10	Has compassion on his people; guides and leads his people
Isaiah 63:15	Watches
Matthew 25:34	Gives his people their inheritance
Mark 11:25–26	Forgives sins

Acts 7:49	Builds his house
Acts 7:54–56	Is in his glory with Jesus
Romans 1:18–19	Reveals his wrath against the wicked
1 Corinthians 2:9	Prepares inconceivable things for those who love him
Colossians 3:1–4	Rules with Christ
Hebrews 8:1–2	Set up the sanctuary, the true tabernacle
Hebrews 11:15–16	Is preparing a city for his people
Hebrews 12:22–24	Judges
Revelation 3:12	Will send down the New Jerusalem from heaven
Revelation 3:21	Sits on his throne
Revelation 5:11–13	Reigns in power; receives worship
Revelation 7:13–17	Shelters those in heaven; wipes away tears
Revelation 21:4–8	Will wipe away tears; dwells among his people
Revelation 22:1–3	Reigns on his throne; provides light

What Will We Find in Heaven?

Psalm 103:19	God's throne
John 14:1–4	Many rooms
Hebrews 8:1–2	God's throne
Revelation 3:12	The city of God, the New Jerusalem, which will descend out of heaven from God
Revelation 3:21	Throne
Revelation 4:2	Throne with someone sitting on it
Revelation 5:11–13	Voice of angels; an encircled throne
Revelation 7:13–17	Throne; temple; living water
Revelation 21:18–21	Wall of city made of precious stone; gates made of pearls; city and street made of gold
Revelation 22:1–3	River of the Water of Life; the Tree of Life on either side of the river; no more night; throne of God and of the Lamb
Revelation 22:13	City gates; Tree of Life

What Will We Do in Heaven?

Nehemiah 9:6	Worship the Lord
Psalm 16:9–11	Rejoice in God's presence; enjoy eternal pleasures

Psalm 23:6	Dwell in the house of the Lord forever
Isaiah 6:2–4	Worship God
Isaiah 49:10	Never hunger or thirst
Daniel 12:2	Live forever
Matthew 5:11–12	Be rewarded
Matthew 25:34	Receive inheritance
John 14:1–4	Live with Jesus
Colossians 3:1–4	Appear with Christ in glory
1 Thessalonians 4:17	Be with the Lord forever
Revelation 3:21	Sit on a throne
Revelation 5:11–13	Praise and worship the Lord
Revelation 7:13–17	Serve God day and night; remain in God's presence; never hunger or thirst
Revelation 21:4–8	Dwell with God; never experience death, mourning, crying, or pain
Revelation 22:1–3	Serve God; see God's face; bear God's name on our foreheads; reign with God forever

Who Lives in Heaven?

Nehemiah 9:6	Multitudes
Psalm 20:6	God
Psalm 33:13–14	God
Psalm 121:1–2	The Maker of heaven and earth
Ecclesiastes 5:2	God
Isaiah 6:2–4	Seraphim
Isaiah 57:15	The exalted One; those who are contrite in spirit
Matthew 5:3	The poor in spirit
Matthew 5:11–12	Those who are persecuted because of Christ
Matthew 5:19–20	Those who practice and teach Jesus' commands
Matthew 6:9–13	God the Father
Matthew 18:10	Angels; the Father
Matthew 18:14	Our Father
Matthew 25:34	The Father; Christ, the King
Mark 11:25–26	Father in heaven
Mark 16:19	Jesus
John 3:11–13	Jesus, the Son of Man

John 6:50–51	Jesus, the Bread of Life
John 14:1–4	The Father; Jesus; those who believe in Jesus
Acts 7:54–56	God; Jesus, the Son of Man
1 Corinthians 15:50	Spiritual bodies
2 Corinthians 5:8	The Lord
Philippians 1:22–23	Jesus
Colossians 3:1–4	Jesus
1 Thessalonians 4:17	The Lord
Hebrews 8:1–2	Jesus, our Great High Priest; God, the Majesty
Hebrews 11:15–16	God's people
Hebrews 12:22–24	Thousands upon thousands of angels; those who have been made righteous; God, the Judge of all; Jesus, the Mediator of a new covenant
Revelation 3:12	Those who are victorious
Revelation 3:21	Those who are victorious; Jesus; the Father
Revelation 5:11–13	Thousands upon thousands of angels; living creatures; elders; God, who sits on the throne; the Lamb
Revelation 7:13–17	Elders; those who have come out of the Great Tribulation; the Lamb
Revelation 8:1	Jesus, the Lamb
Revelation 12:7–9	Michael, the archangel, and his angels; the dragon and his angels, who are hurled to the earth
Revelation 21:4–8	God and his people
Revelation 22:1–3	Angels; Lamb of God; God's servants
Revelation 22:13	Jesus, the Alpha and Omega

What Does Jesus Do in Heaven?

Matthew 25:34	Reigns as King
Mark 16:19	Sits at the right hand of God
John 14:1–4	Prepares a place for his people
Acts 7:54–56	Stands at the right hand of God
Colossians 3:1–4	Sits at the right hand of God
Hebrews 7:25	Saves those who come to God through him; intercedes for the saints
Hebrews 8:1–2	Serves in the sanctuary as our Great High Priest

Hebrews 12:22–24	Mediates a new covenant between God and his people
Revelation 2:7	Gives the right to eat from the Tree of Life
Revelation 3:12	Makes the victorious a pillar in the temple of God; writes his name on the city and his people
Revelation 3:21	Gives the victorious the right to sit with him on his throne
Revelation 5:11–13	Receives honor, praise, and glory
Revelation 7:13–17	Shelters those made clean; shepherds them and leads them to springs of living water
Revelation 8:1	Opens a scroll with seven seals
Revelation 22:1–3	Reigns on his throne

HELL

How Does the Bible Describe Hell?

2 Samuel 22:5–6	Overwhelming destruction; coiling cords of the grave; snares of death
Job 17:16	Gates of death
Psalm 49:13–14	Death; decay
Proverbs 23:13–14	Death
Ecclesiastes 9:10	No work, planning, knowledge, or wisdom
Isaiah 66:24	Worms that don't die and eat dead bodies; unquenchable fire
Jeremiah 7:31	Fire
Daniel 12:2–3	Shame; everlasting contempt
Matthew 3:12	Burnt chaff; unquenchable fire
Matthew 5:22	Judgment; fire
Matthew 10:28	Destruction of body and soul
Matthew 13:41–42	Blazing furnace; weeping and gnashing of teeth
Matthew 13:49–50	Blazing furnace; weeping and gnashing of teeth
Matthew 16:18	Gates of hades
Matthew 25:41	Eternal fire
Matthew 25:46	Place of eternal punishment
Mark 9:43	Fire that never goes out
Mark 9:47–48	Unquenchable fire; worms

Luke 16:23–25	Fire; heat; agony
Acts 2:29–31	Decay; abandonment
Romans 2:6–8	Wrath; anger
1 Corinthians 15:55	Death
2 Thessalonians 1:6–9	Everlasting destruction
James 3:6	Fire
2 Peter 2:4, 9	Chains of darkness; judgment
Jude v. 7	Eternal fire
Revelation 1:18	Jesus holds the keys of death/hell
Revelation 14:11	Smoke of torment
Revelation 19:20	Fiery lake of burning sulfur
Revelation 20:10	Lake of burning sulfur
Revelation 20:15	Lake of fire
Revelation 21:8	Lake of burning sulfur; the second death

Where Is Hell?

Genesis 37:34–35	The grave
Numbers 16:33	Down; the realm of the dead
1 Samuel 2:6	Down; the grave
2 Samuel 22:5–6	The grave
Job 17:16	Down; in the dust
Psalm 6:5	The grave
Psalm 9:17	Down; the realm of the dead
Psalm 49:13–14	The grave; far from princely mansions
Psalm 139:8	In the depths
Proverbs 15:24	Down; the realm of the dead
Ecclesiastes 9:10	The realm of the dead
Ezekiel 31:16	Down; the realm of the dead; the pit
Matthew 25:41	Separate from Christ
Luke 10:15	Down; hades
Luke 16:23–25	Hades
Acts 2:29–31	Realm of the dead
2 Thessalonians 1:6–9	Away from the presence of God
Revelation 1:18	Hades

Who Is in Hell?

Psalm 6:5	The dead; those who do not proclaim the Lord's name
Psalm 9:17	The wicked; nations that forget God
Psalm 49:13–14	Those who trust in themselves, and those who follow them
Isaiah 66:24	Those who rebel against God
Matthew 5:22	Those who do not repent of anger toward a brother or sister
Matthew 10:28	Those who are sentenced to destruction by God
Matthew 13:41–42	All who do evil
Matthew 13:49–50	The wicked
Matthew 23:33–34	Religious leaders whose hearts are far from the Lord; those who persecute God's prophets and teachers
Matthew 25:41	The cursed; the Devil and his angels
Mark 9:47–48	Those who lust
Romans 2:6–8	The self-seeking; those who reject truth and follow evil
2 Thessalonians 1:6–9	Those who do not know the Lord or obey the gospel of Christ
2 Peter 2:4, 9	Angels who sin; the unrighteous
Jude v. 7	The sexually immoral
Revelation 14:11	Those who worship the Beast or receive the mark of its name
Revelation 19:20	The Beast and the False Prophet; those who receive the mark of the Beast and worship its image
Revelation 20:10	The Devil; the Beast; the False Prophet
Revelation 20:15	Anyone whose name is not written in the Book of Life
Revelation 21:8	Cowards; unbelievers; the vile; murderers; the sexually immoral; those who practice magic arts; idolaters; liars

What Happens to People in Hell?

Numbers 16:33	Perish
1 Samuel 2:6	Brought down to the grave

2 Samuel 22:5–6	Overwhelmed by death and destruction; surrounded by cords of the grave; confronted by the snares of death
Job 17:16	Descend into the dust
Psalm 6:5	No one praises the Lord's name
Psalm 9:17	Have forgotten God
Psalm 49:13–14	Destined for death; bodies decay in the grave
Proverbs 15:24	Descend to the realm of the dead
Ecclesiastes 9:10	Be without work, planning, knowledge, or wisdom
Isaiah 66:24	Their dead bodies are eaten by worms that never die and burned in an unquenchable fire
Daniel 12:2–3	Receive shame and everlasting contempt
Matthew 3:12	Burn like chaff
Matthew 5:22	Subject to judgment of fire
Matthew 10:28	Body and soul are destroyed
Matthew 13:41–42	Thrown into the blazing furnace by Jesus' angels
Matthew 13:49–50	Thrown into the blazing furnace by angels
Matthew 23:33–34	Receive condemnation
Matthew 25:41	Separated from Christ; cursed; thrown into the eternal fire
Matthew 25:46	Receive eternal punishment
Mark 9:47–48	Eaten by worms in an unquenchable fire
Luke 16:23–25	Tormented; suffer heat, thirst, and agony
Acts 2:29–31	Decay; are abandoned
Romans 2:6–8	Receive God's wrath and anger as a repayment for sin
1 Corinthians 15:55	Suffer death
2 Peter 2:4, 9	Chained; held for judgment and punishment
Jude v. 7	Punished with eternal fire
Revelation 14:11	Tormented; receive no rest, day or night
Revelation 19:20	Thrown alive into burning sulfur
Revelation 20:10	Tormented day and night, forever
Revelation 20:15	Thrown into the lake of fire
Revelation 21:8	Experience the second death; thrown into the lake of burning sulfur